# Bon Appétit~Without the Wheat

# Bon Appétit~Without the Wheat

## Gluten-free recipes from appetizers to desserts

**Julie Ambrose**

Infinity Publishing

**ISBN 0-7414-4071-7**

*Front cover, back cover and author photograph by Steve Reed- Tradewinds Images, Stockbridge, NY.*

*All other photos by Julie Ambrose.*

**Published by:**

**INFI∞ITY**
PUBLISHING.COM
**1094 New Dehaven Street, Suite 100**
**West Conshohocken, PA 19428-2713**
**Info@buybooksontheweb.com**
**www.buybooksontheweb.com**
**Toll-free (877) BUY BOOK**
**Local Phone (610) 941-9999**
**Fax (610) 941-9959**

*Printed in the United States of America*
*Printed on Recycled Paper*
*Published June 2007*

*For my husband, Matt*

*For taking me to every doctor appointment, for making me every flavor of Jell-O,*
*for cleaning up every kitchen mess, for trying every recipe and*
*for everything else you do every day.*

# Foreword

I grew up cooking. We cooked everything from weekday dinners to fancy dinner parties and holiday celebrations. I loved the aromas, the tastes, and the gathering of family and friends around the table to share. Julie's book brings back all those wonderful memories. Reviewing the recipes in this book was like walking back into our family kitchen, but with a fabulous gluten free twist. There are those tried and true favorites, the healthy standbys, and even those special occasion recipes for fun! Julie has carefully crafted both the familiar favorite recipes and the special dishes into delicious gluten free wonders. I hope you enjoy the recipes as much as I did!

Indeed a wheat-less Bon Appétit!

Anne Roland Lee, MSEd, RD, CDN
Nutritionist, Celiac Disease Center at Columbia University

# Contents

# Introduction

## Bon appétit
*an exclamation used to wish someone an enjoyable meal;*
*good appetite; enjoy your meal*

Enjoying a good meal is not usually a source of stress for most people. In fact, some of the most memorable events in our lives involve eating. How do we celebrate a birthday, a promotion, or a wedding? It's usually with food. Our scrapbooks are filled with photos of barbeques and bake sales, wedding cakes and piles of Halloween candy. For the other days, sometimes eating a meal is the only chance we get to sit down, relax and catch up with our family and friends.

That's the way I thought about food for most of my life. Or, to be more exact, I didn't really think about food that much at all. It was just there. I ate what I liked, I tried to eat healthy, but I never realized what a huge part of our time is spent thinking about, preparing and eating food.

Then I began to get sick. I went to emergency rooms, doctors, gastroenterologists, and even an acupuncturist. While I was waiting for appointments with doctors and test results to come back, my symptoms were getting worse. I started looking at food in a different way. It was anything but enjoyable to eat. Every meal was a struggle; knowing I had to eat, but also knowing how I was going to feel when I was done. Each doctor I saw eliminated something from my diet, including fats, dairy, caffeine, meats and citrus. In one month I ate 34 boxes of Jell-O and not much else because my diet had become so limited. I began resenting food, not to mention the rest of the world, who seemed to be taking so much pleasure in eating. Not only was I missing out on the nutrients from food, but I was missing out on all the other things that go along with enjoying a good meal. There were times that I decided to eat what I wanted and suffer through anything that followed. Five minutes later, I was angry at what I had done to myself. So, this is how I began to relate to food, as something I needed, but definitely not something I enjoyed.

Months went by, and I got to experience every bizarre test ever invented. Most of the tests came back with normal results and I was told to try eliminating another food or ingredient or given another prescription to fill. In 3 months I had countless blood and urine tests, a chest x-ray, an ultrasound, a CT scan, an MRI, 2 gallbladder HIDA scans, a gastric emptying study, a barium swallow and lower GI series, 2 endoscopies, and a colonoscopy. These 3 months also included 2 weeks in the hospital on a clear liquid diet (I was given a cheeseburger by one of my doctors to

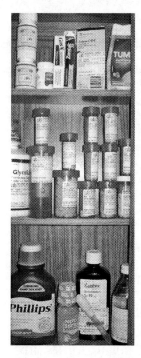

"see what happens"). It was finally determined that my gallbladder was not functioning and I should have it removed. After my surgery was done and I didn't feel any better, I began a new hobby to distract myself from eating. I diagnosed myself with every rare and fatal disease on the internet by typing in my symptoms and the results of the various tests I had taken. I came to the conclusion that I must be the only one going through this, and therefore, the disease shall be named after me, or a name of my choice. During the time I was sick, my medicine cabinet was full of all types of medications. Each one had their own directions and side effects.

With a genetic screening, I was eventually diagnosed with celiac disease after 11 months. Although it seems like forever when you aren't able to eat, I was actually pretty fortunate. The average length of time to diagnose celiac disease is 8-11 years. Although it was a frustrating time, I don't think that my doctors could have diagnosed me any faster. I was tested for antibodies to diagnose celiac disease with blood work in the beginning, but I had also been on a clear liquid diet for many weeks prior to the test, so this test came back negative. When I got my "official" diagnosis after having the genetic test, I stood at the local health food store, stunned at the strange ingredients and high prices. I was happy to have a possible explanation to my problem, but I immediately began to list all of the foods I would never be able to eat again. I also had an explanation why the saltine crackers, burnt toast and medications (and cheeseburgers!) were making me even sicker. I started learning about "hidden gluten" and "cross-contamination". If it wasn't bad enough that I would need to avoid cookies, cake, pasta and bread, I also found out that gluten is everywhere. It is added to almost everything. And, if it's not added, my food could be contaminated by gluten by being processed in the same facility or prepared in the same kitchen. I did try to see the positive: that I didn't need any more medications or surgeries or lengthy hospital visits, and I would be feeling better in a couple days. Gluten-free shopping list in-hand, I began trying new foods and trying to remake my old favorites. I learned that if you do something three times a day, everyday, you will get the hang of it faster than you think.

So, now I know what I can and can't eat – or at least how to find out. I had learned where to go shopping and how to safely prepare my food. The only difficult part for me is when I'm not at home and it's gets a little tricky to enjoy a meal. What do you do when your co-workers are eating pizza, your family is having birthday cake or your friends invite you to dinner? I wish I had some wonderful advice on how to get a waitress to understand what gluten is or what cross-contamination means, but I still get a bit nervous about eating somewhere unknown. I hope that eventually that will be as easy as saying you are a diabetic or have a peanut allergy. I am guilty of avoiding restaurants that do not specifically indicate they have a gluten-free menu. Sometimes I worry about someone thinking that I'm being difficult or that I'm on some fad diet, and a lot of the time I just don't feel like explaining it all over again. But, maybe if we explain our situation (and there are enough requests), we would be pleasantly surprised. Of course, the easiest situations are the times when I can bring my own food to share and maybe even tell someone about celiac disease while I'm at it.  But, there will be many times when we just can't bring our own gluten-free goodies and making a special request is not an option.  It's easy to feel left out and curse the Gluten Gods, but it's also a good time to remember that there is probably another reason that you are gathered together with these people other than food.  If that weren't true, we would just invite random strangers to our weddings, birthdays and into our homes for Thanksgiving dinner.

I have gone on a year-long journey that I was not expecting. Today I am still learning about celiac disease, trying new recipes and adapting to a new way of looking at food.  Since my diagnosis, I have only had one medical test (a standard bone density screening) and my medicine cabinet is completely empty.  Dealing with celiac disease not only changed the way I looked at food but also changed the way I look at many things in life.  It is easy to take for granted the days we are able to eat and enjoy social events without worry.  It is sometimes difficult to put things in perspective and not let every meal or event be about celiac disease.  I know that not a day goes by when I'm not forced to be reminded of this strange illness I have.  The first 100 times I was asked "What do you eat anyway?" I really didn't have a very appetizing answer.  But I have slowly replaced most of my favorite foods with gluten-free versions and it has helped to feel like this isn't such a huge disruption in my life.  Although it is overwhelming at first, we all become experts at deciphering labels, ordering meals and being creative in the kitchen.  I hope that this book will make it easier for those of you with celiac disease, a wheat allergy or your friends and family to prepare your favorite foods.  Beyond health and happiness, I hope that you are able to enjoy a gluten-free meal without worry. Bon Appétit!

*"One of the most sublime experiences we can ever have is to wake up feeling healthy after we have been sick."*

*~Rabbi Harold Kushner*

*"The ambition of every good cook must be to make something very good with the fewest possible ingredients."*

*~Urbain Dubois*

# Author's Note

The purpose of this cookbook was to make gluten-free cooking and baking as "normal" as possible. I have found that many recipes, although very good, were very complicated to make. It's not always easy to find all of the different flours and ingredients, or to store them all according to their own individual requirements. When I hear about families that are making two meals: one gluten-free and one regular, it is disappointing. Besides being so much extra work, it seems like the chances of cross-contamination would be greatly increased. However, if so many people are going to the trouble to prepare two meals, it must be for a good reason. The added cost and the unusual taste of gluten-free food are usually the most common reasons for the extra effort. Both of these problems are lessened by using more common ingredients and relying less on prepackaged items. The two main specialty ingredients I have used in this cookbook are gluten-free flour and xanthan gum.

Gluten-free flour: For all recipes in this book I used either *Bob's Red Mill Gluten Free All Purpose Baking Flour* or *Gluten-Free Pantry – Beth's All Purpose Baking Flour*. Either flour can be used interchangeably (unless noted in the recipe) and are usually available at most health food stores and some supermarkets. Both flours can be purchased in bulk online to save money.

Xanthan gum: Used in gluten-free baking to bind ingredients together and to replace some of the elastic properties of gluten. It is expensive, but a little goes a long way. All of the xanthan gum amounts in this book have been calculated, but a general rule for use is:

Breads: 1 teaspoon per 1 cup GF flour

Cakes: ½ teaspoon per 1 cup GF flour

Cookies: ¼ teaspoon per 1 cup GF flour

All other ingredients labeled gluten-free in this book are readily available at most grocery stores. (For example: GF chocolate chips, GF vanilla). They are ingredients that sometimes contain gluten and should be checked **every** time they are purchased.

# Celiac Disease

*From the Celiac Disease Awareness Campaign*

National Institute of Diabetes and Digestive and Kidney Diseases (NIDDK)

National Institutes of Health

## What is celiac disease?

Celiac disease is a digestive disease that damages the small intestine and interferes with absorption of nutrients from food. People who have celiac disease cannot tolerate a protein called gluten, found in wheat, rye, and barley. Gluten is found mainly in foods, but is also found in products we use every day, such as stamp and envelope adhesive, medicines, and vitamins.

When people with celiac disease eat foods or use products containing gluten, their immune system responds by damaging the small intestine. The tiny, fingerlike protrusions lining the small intestine are damaged or destroyed. Called villi, they normally allow nutrients from food to be absorbed into the bloodstream. Without healthy villi, a person becomes malnourished, regardless of the quantity of food eaten.

Because the body's own immune system causes the damage, celiac disease is considered an autoimmune disorder. However, it is also classified as a disease of malabsorption because nutrients are not absorbed. Celiac disease is also known as celiac sprue, nontropical sprue, and gluten-sensitive enteropathy.

Celiac disease is a genetic disease, meaning it runs in families. Sometimes the disease is triggered-or becomes active for the first time-after surgery, pregnancy, childbirth, viral infection, or severe emotional stress.

## What are the symptoms of celiac disease?

Celiac disease affects people differently. Symptoms may occur in the digestive system, or in other parts of the body. For example, one person might have diarrhea and abdominal pain, while another person may be irritable or depressed. In fact, irritability is one of the most common symptoms in children.

Symptoms of celiac disease may include one or more of the following:

- gas
- recurring abdominal bloating and pain
- chronic diarrhea
- pale, foul-smelling, or fatty stool
- weight loss / weight gain
- fatigue
- unexplained anemia (a low count of red blood cells causing fatigue)
- bone or joint pain
- osteoporosis, osteopenia
- behavioral changes
- tingling numbness in the legs (from nerve damage)
- muscle cramps
- seizures
- missed menstrual periods (often because of excessive weight loss)
- infertility, recurrent miscarriage
- delayed growth
- failure to thrive in infants
- pale sores inside the mouth, called aphthous ulcers
- tooth discoloration or loss of enamel
- itchy skin rash called dermatitis herpetiformis

A person with celiac disease may have no symptoms. People without symptoms are still at risk for the complications of celiac disease, including malnutrition. The longer a person goes undiagnosed and untreated, the greater the chance of developing malnutrition and other complications. Anemia, delayed growth, and weight loss are signs of malnutrition: The body is just not getting enough nutrients. Malnutrition is a serious problem for children because they need adequate nutrition to develop properly.

## Why are celiac symptoms so varied?

Researchers are studying the reasons celiac disease affects people differently. Some people develop symptoms as children, others as adults. Some people with celiac disease may not have symptoms, while others may not know their symptoms are from celiac disease. The undamaged part of their small intestine may not be able to absorb enough nutrients to prevent symptoms.

The length of time a person is breastfed, the age a person started eating gluten-containing foods, and the amount of gluten containing foods one eats are three factors thought to play a role in when and how celiac appears. Some studies have shown, for example, that the longer a person was breastfed, the later the symptoms of celiac disease appear and the more uncommon the symptoms.

## How is celiac disease diagnosed?

Recognizing celiac disease can be difficult because some of its symptoms are similar to those of other diseases. In fact, sometimes celiac disease is confused with irritable bowel syndrome, iron-deficiency anemia caused by menstrual blood loss, Crohn's disease, diverticulitis, intestinal infections, and chronic fatigue syndrome. As a result, celiac disease is commonly under diagnosed or misdiagnosed.

Recently, researchers discovered that people with celiac disease have higher than normal levels of certain autoantibodies in their blood. Antibodies are protective proteins produced by the immune system in response to substances that the body perceives to be threatening. Autoantibodies are proteins that react against the body's own molecules or tissues. To diagnose celiac disease, physicians will usually test blood to measure levels of

- Immunoglobulin A (IgA)
- anti-tissue transglutaminase (tTGA)
- IgA anti-endomysium antibodies (AEA)

Before being tested, one should continue to eat a regular diet that includes foods with gluten, such as breads and pastas. If a person stops eating foods with gluten before being tested, the results may be negative for celiac disease even if celiac disease is actually present.

If the tests and symptoms suggest celiac disease, the doctor will perform a small bowel biopsy. During the biopsy, the doctor removes a tiny piece of tissue from the small intestine to check for damage to the villi. To obtain the tissue sample, the doctor eases a long, thin tube called an endoscope through the mouth and stomach into the small intestine. Using instruments passed through the endoscope, the doctor then takes the sample.

When the diagnosis of celiac disease is uncertain because of indeterminate results, testing for certain genetic markers (HLA haplotypes) can stratify individuals to high or low risk for celiac disease. Greater than 97 percent of celiac disease individuals have the DQ2 and/or DQ8 marker, compared to about 40 percent of the general population. Therefore, an individual negative for DQ2 or DQ8 is extremely unlikely to have celiac disease (high negative predictive value).

For individuals who have been placed on a gluten-free diet without an appropriate diagnostic evaluation, testing should follow a gluten challenge. For those who decline to undergo a gluten challenge, the absence of DQ2 and DQ8 by HLA typing may help exclude the diagnosis. Resolution of symptoms on a gluten-free diet is not sufficient to diagnose celiac disease; however, there are no adverse nutritional outcomes associated with a carefully planned gluten-free diet.

## Screening

Screening for celiac disease involves testing for the presence of antibodies in the blood in people without symptoms. Americans are not routinely screened for celiac disease. Testing for celiac-related antibodies in children less than 5 years old may not be reliable. However, since celiac disease is hereditary, family members, particularly first-degree relatives-meaning parents, siblings, or children of people who have been diagnosed-may wish to be tested for the disease. About 5 to 15 percent of an affected person's first-degree relatives will also have the disease. About 3 to 8 percent of people with type 1 diabetes will have biopsy-confirmed celiac disease and 5 to 10 percent of people with Down syndrome will be diagnosed with celiac disease.

# What is the treatment?

The only treatment for celiac disease is to follow a gluten-free diet. When a person is first diagnosed with celiac disease, the doctor usually will ask the person to work with a dietitian on a gluten-free diet plan. A dietitian is a health care professional who specializes in food and nutrition. Someone with celiac disease can learn from a dietitian how to read ingredient lists and identify foods that contain gluten in order to make informed decisions at the grocery store and when eating out.

For most people, following this diet will stop symptoms, heal existing intestinal damage, and prevent further damage. Improvements begin within days of starting the diet. The small intestine is usually completely healed in 3 to 6 months in children and younger adults and within 2 years for older adults. Healed means a person now has villi that can absorb nutrients from food into the bloodstream.

**In order to stay well, people with celiac disease must avoid gluten for the rest of their lives. Eating any gluten, no matter how small an amount, can damage the small intestine**. The damage will occur in anyone with the disease, including people without noticeable symptoms. Depending on a person's age at diagnosis, some problems will not improve, such as delayed growth and tooth discoloration.

Some people with celiac disease show no improvement on the gluten-free diet. The condition is called unresponsive celiac disease. The most common reason for poor response is that small amounts of gluten are still present in the diet. Advice from a dietitian who is skilled in educating patients about the gluten-free diet is essential to achieve best results.

Rarely, the intestinal injury will continue despite a strictly gluten-free diet. People in this situation have severely damaged intestines that cannot heal. Because their intestines are not absorbing enough nutrients, they may need to directly receive nutrients into their bloodstream through a vein (intravenously). People with this condition may need to be evaluated for complications of the disease. Researchers are now evaluating drug treatments for unresponsive celiac disease.

# The Gluten-Free Diet

A gluten-free diet means not eating foods that contain wheat (including spelt, triticale, and kamut), rye, and barley. The foods and products made from these grains are also not allowed. In other words, a person with celiac disease should not eat most grain, pasta, cereal, and many processed foods. Despite these restrictions, people with celiac disease can eat a well balanced diet with a variety of foods, including gluten-free bread and pasta. For example, people with celiac disease can use potato, rice, soy, amaranth, quinoa, buckwheat, or bean flour instead of wheat flour. They can buy gluten-free bread, pasta, and other products from stores that carry organic foods, or order products from special food companies. Gluten-free products are increasingly available from regular stores.

Checking labels for "gluten free" is important since many corn and rice products are produced in factories that also manufacture wheat products. Hidden sources of gluten include additives such as modified food starch, preservatives, and stabilizers. Wheat and wheat products are often used as thickeners, stabilizers, and texture enhancers in foods.

"Plain" meat, fish, rice, fruits, and vegetables do not contain gluten, so people with celiac disease can eat as much of these foods as they like. Recommending that people with celiac disease avoid oats is controversial because some people have been able to eat oats without having symptoms. Scientists are currently studying whether people with celiac disease can tolerate oats. Until the studies are complete, people with celiac disease should follow their physician's or dietitian's advice about eating oats.

The gluten-free diet is challenging. It requires a completely new approach to eating that affects a person's entire life. Newly diagnosed people and their families may find support groups to be particularly helpful as they learn to adjust to a new way of life. People with celiac disease have to be extremely careful about what they buy for lunch at school or work, what they purchase at the grocery store, what they eat at restaurants or parties, or what they grab for a snack. Eating out can be a challenge. If a person with celiac disease is in doubt about a menu item, ask the waiter or chef about ingredients and preparation, or if a gluten-free menu is available.

Gluten is also used in some medications. One should check with the pharmacist to learn whether medications used contain gluten. Since gluten is also sometimes used as an additive in unexpected products, it is important to read all labels. If the ingredients are not listed on the product label, the manufacturer of the product should provide the list upon request. With practice, screening for gluten becomes second nature.

# What are the complications of celiac disease?

Damage to the small intestine and the resulting nutrient absorption problems put a person with celiac disease at risk for malnutrition and anemia as well as several diseases and health problems.

- **Lymphoma and adenocarcinoma** are cancers that can develop in the intestine.
- **Osteoporosis** is a condition in which the bones become weak, brittle, and prone to breaking. Poor calcium absorption contributes to osteoporosis.
- **Miscarriage and congenital malformation** of the baby, such as neural tube defects, are risks for pregnant women with untreated celiac disease because of nutrient absorption problems.
- **Short stature** refers to being significantly under-the-average height. Short stature results when childhood celiac disease prevents nutrient absorption during the years when nutrition is critical to a child's normal growth and development. Children who are diagnosed and treated before their growth stops may have a catch-up period.

# How common is celiac disease?

Data on the prevalence of celiac disease is spotty. In Italy, about 1 in 250 people and in Ireland about 1 in 300 people have celiac disease. Recent studies have shown that it may be more common in Africa, South America, and Asia than previously believed.

Until recently, celiac disease was thought to be uncommon in the United States. However, studies have shown that celiac disease is very common. Recent findings estimate about 2 million people in the United States have celiac disease, or about 1 in 133 people. Among people who have a first-degree relative diagnosed with celiac disease, as many as 1 in 22 people may have the disease.

Celiac disease could be under diagnosed in the United States for a number of reasons including:

- Celiac symptoms can be attributed to other problems.
- Many doctors are not knowledgeable about the disease.
- Only a small number of U.S. laboratories are experienced and skilled in testing for celiac disease.

More research is needed to learn the true prevalence of celiac disease among Americans.

# Diseases Linked to Celiac Disease

People with celiac disease tend to have other autoimmune diseases. The connection between celiac disease and these diseases may be genetic. These diseases include

- thyroid disease
- systemic lupus erythematosus
- type 1 diabetes
- liver disease
- collagen vascular disease
- rheumatoid arthritis
- Sjögren's syndrome

# Dermatitis Herpetiformis

Dermatitis herpetiformis (DH) is a severe itchy, blistering manifestation of celiac disease. The rash usually occurs on the elbows, knees, and buttocks. Not all people with celiac disease develop dermatitis herpetiformis. Unlike other forms of celiac disease, the range of intestinal abnormalities in DH is highly variable, from minimal to severe. Only about 20 percent of people with DH have intestinal symptoms of celiac disease.

To diagnose DH, the doctor will test the person's blood for autoantibodies related to celiac disease and will biopsy the person's skin. If the antibody tests are positive and the skin biopsy has the typical findings of DH, patients do not need to have an intestinal biopsy. Both the skin disease and the intestinal disease respond to gluten-free diet and recur if gluten is added back into diet. In addition, the rash symptoms can be controlled with medications such as dapsone (4',4'diamino-diphenylsuphone). However, dapsone does not treat the intestinal condition and people with DH should also maintain a gluten-free diet.

# Hope Through Research

The National Institute of Diabetes and Digestive and Kidney Diseases (NIDDK) conducts and supports research on celiac disease. NIDDK-supported researchers are studying the genetic and environmental causes of celiac disease. In addition, researchers are studying the substances found in gluten that are believed to be responsible for the destruction of the immune system function, as happens in celiac disease. They are engineering enzymes designed to destroy these immunotoxic peptides. Researchers are also developing educational materials for standardized medical training to raise awareness among healthcare providers. The hope is that increased understanding and awareness will lead to earlier diagnosis and treatment of celiac disease.

# Points to Remember

- People with celiac disease cannot tolerate gluten, a protein in wheat, rye, barley, and possibly oats.
- Celiac disease damages the small intestine and interferes with nutrient absorption.
- Without treatment, people with celiac disease can develop complications like cancer, osteoporosis, anemia, and seizures.
- A person with celiac disease may or may not have symptoms.
- Diagnosis involves blood tests and a biopsy of the small intestine.
- Since celiac disease is hereditary, family members of a person with celiac disease may wish to be tested.
- Celiac disease is treated by eliminating all gluten from the diet. The gluten-free diet is a lifetime requirement.
- A dietitian can teach a person with celiac disease food selection, label reading, and other strategies to help manage the disease.

The following are six key elements in the management of individuals affected by celiac disease:

Consultation with a skilled dietitian

Education about the disease

Lifelong adherence to a gluten-free diet

Identification and treatment of nutritional deficiencies

Access to an advocacy group

Continuous long-term follow-up by a multidisciplinary team

*"One cannot think well, love well, sleep well, if one has not dined well."*

*~Virginia Wolfe*

# Appetizers

# Olive Tapenade

1 cup black olives, pitted and rinsed

1 cup green olives (preferably Kalamata), pitted and rinsed

1 clove garlic, minced

½ cup olive oil

½ tablespoon lemon juice

1 tablespoon capers

1 teaspoon anchovy paste (optional)

¼ teaspoon pepper

Add olives, garlic, capers and anchovy paste to food processor or blender.  Add olive oil slowly.  Add lemon juice and pepper to taste.  Keep refrigerated.

You may use any combination of olives you like, including an all black or all green olive tapenade.

# Mango Salsa

3 mangos, chopped*
5-7 fresh chili peppers, seeded and chopped
1 small onion, minced
¼ cup cilantro**
½ teaspoon salt
Juice of 2 limes

Mix all ingredients in a bowl, food processor or blender.  Refrigerate 1-2 hours before serving.

*Can substitute 2 cups chopped nectarines or peaches

**Can substitute ¼ cup fresh parsley

*This recipe is from Barbara Ambrose and Emilio Tobón*

# Stuffed Mushrooms

24 whole large fresh mushrooms

1 cup cooked crab meat or shrimp

1 tablespoon fresh parsley (1 teaspoon dried)

1 teaspoon capers, chopped (optional)

1 small onion, chopped

1 clove garlic, minced

2 tablespoons olive oil

Preheat oven to 350°. Clean mushrooms and remove and discard the stems. In a bowl, combine the seafood, capers, parsley, onion and garlic. Fill each mushroom cap with one tablespoon of the mixture. Lightly spray a baking sheet with GF cooking spray and arrange mushrooms so that they are not touching. Bake for 10-12 minutes or until the mushrooms are cooked through.

*To clean mushrooms, simply brush with a slightly damp paper towel or a soft brush.

# Roasted Red Pepper Dip

1 (7oz.) jar roasted red peppers*
1 cup GF cream cheese
1 clove garlic, minced
Salt & pepper

Coarsely chop roasted red peppers and place in a food processor or blender until smooth. Add cream cheese, garlic, and salt and pepper to taste. Refrigerate 2-3 hours before serving.

*To roast your own red peppers: Under a broiler or grill, cook the whole peppers until they start to blister and are blackened. Remove from heat and seal in a paper bag until cooled. Peel off the skins, cut in half and scrape out the core and seeds. To keep in the refrigerator for 2-3 weeks, place in a jar with minced garlic and cover with olive oil.

# Veggie Dip

1 cup GF mayonnaise*

1 cup GF sour cream*

3 tablespoons grated onion

1 clove garlic, minced

3 tablespoons fresh dill**

Combine all ingredients in food processor or blender until combined.  Chill 3-4 hours before serving.

*Can substitute with 1 cup of plain yogurt or 1 cup cottage cheese pureed in a blender

**Fresh dill is the best in this recipe, but you may also substitute with 3 teaspoons dried dill.

# *Hummus*

1 can (15.5oz.) chic peas (garbanzo beans), drained with liquid reserved

2 cloves garlic, minced

Juice of 1 lemon

1 tablespoon olive oil

¼ teaspoon cumin (optional)

¼ cup Tahini paste-ground sesame seeds (optional)

In a food processor or blender, combine chic peas with ¼ cup of reserved chic pea liquid, garlic, lemon juice, cumin and tahini paste. While mixing, slowly add olive oil.

For roasted red pepper hummus: omit reserved chic pea liquid and add half of a roasted red pepper.

# Guacamole

1 cup mashed avocado

1 tablespoon lemon juice

1 teaspoon salt

2 tablespoons grated onion

1 clove garlic, minced

2 chiles, finely chopped (preferably serrano)

½ cup chopped tomato

2 tablespoons chopped cilantro

Mix all ingredients together in bowl and keep refrigerated until serving. There is no need to use a food processor or blender, as guacamole is generally a bit "lumpy".

For a super quick guacamole: Mix 1 large mashed avocado with ½ cup of your favorite GF salsa and 1 tablespoon lemon juice.

# Spicy Olive Dip

1 (6 oz.) can black olives, chopped

1 (4oz.) can green chiles, diced

2 large tomatoes, finely chopped and seeded

2 tablespoons onion, finely chopped

1 clove garlic, minced

1 tablespoon lime or lemon juice

3 tablespoons olive oil

Salt & pepper to taste

Mix all ingredients well in a medium bowl. Refrigerate before serving. This is a good dip for tortilla chips or vegetables, but can also be used as a spread for hamburgers or sandwiches.

# Blackened Salsa

5 medium tomatoes

1 medium onion, quartered

3 whole cloves garlic, peeled

¼ cup fresh cilantro*

2 teaspoons toasted cumin seeds**

Juice of 1 lime

2-3 chiles in adobo sauce***

Set oven to broil. Place whole tomatoes and quartered onion on a baking sheet. Broil until blackened and juices run from tomatoes for approximately 30 minutes. Add whole cloves of garlic and broil an additional 5 minutes. In a food processor or blender process the chiles, cilantro, lime juice, onion, cumin and garlic. Add half of the tomato at a time and pulse until just mixed. Pour into glass canning jar while still hot. Refrigerate. This keeps well for 2-3 weeks.

*Can substitute with ¼ cup fresh parsley

**Can substitute with 1 teaspoon dried cumin

***Can substitute with seeded jalapeño peppers or your choice of favorite hot peppers

*This recipe is from Barbara Ambrose and Emilio Tobón*

# Cucumber Dip

1 medium cucumber, finely chopped

1 clove garlic, minced

8 scallions, finely chopped

2 cups plain yogurt or GF sour cream*

¼ fresh chopped dill or mint (optional)

Salt & pepper

Mix cucumber, garlic, herbs and scallions with yogurt or sour cream in a medium bowl. Season with salt and pepper. Keep refrigerated.

*Can substitute with 14 oz. firm tofu

# Jalapeño Poppers

1 (12oz.) jar jalapeño peppers, drained or about 20 fresh jalapeños*

1 (3oz.) package GF cream cheese, softened

½ cup shredded cheddar cheese

10 GF bacon strips, cut in half (optional)

Preheat oven to 375˚. Slit peppers lengthwise down one side, leaving the stem intact. Scrape out seeds and veins. With or a mixer or by hand, beat together cheddar cheese with cream cheese. Fill each pepper with a teaspoon of cheese mix. Wrap with half of a bacon strip. Hold together with a toothpick if needed. Arrange cheese side up on a baking sheet. Bake 6-8 minutes or until cheese is melted. Best served warm.

You can also cook the bacon ahead of time and mix the crumbled pieces with the cheeses.

It is usually a good idea to wear rubber gloves while handling and cleaning the peppers.

# *Tabbouleh*

1 cup quinoa*

2 cups water

2 tomatoes, seeded and chopped

1 medium cucumber, diced

¼ cup finely chopped scallions

1/3 cup lemon juice

2 tablespoons olive oil

4 tablespoons fresh mint

4 tablespoons parsley

½ teaspoon salt

¼ teaspoon pepper

In a medium saucepan bring the quinoa and water to a boil. Cover and reduce heat to low. Simmer for 15 minutes. Remove from heat and allow quinoa to cool. Combine remaining ingredients in a large bowl until well combined. Fluff the quinoa with a fork and mix in with other ingredients.

*Before using quinoa, rinse well in cold water.

# Fruit Dip

1 cup plain yogurt or firm silken tofu

1 medium ripe banana

1 tablespoon honey

¼ teaspoon cinnamon

¼ cup orange juice

2 tablespoons chopped nuts (optional)

Mix all ingredients together in a medium bowl.  Refrigerate 2-4 hours.  Serve with your favorite fruits- strawberries, melon, pineapple, apples or peaches placed on a bamboo skewer.

# Eggplant Dip

2 medium eggplants

1 clove garlic, minced

1 tablespoon lemon juice

¼ teaspoon red pepper flakes (optional)

Salt & pepper

Preheat oven to 350°. Bake whole eggplants on a baking sheet for 40 minutes or until tender. Remove and cool. Slice lengthwise. Scoop out flesh and mix with remaining ingredients. Mix together with a fork, potato masher or in a blender or food processor if you prefer a smoother dip. Chill at least 30 minutes. Serve with vegetables, GF crackers or corn chips.

# Spinach and Artichoke Dip

1 (4oz.) can diced green chiles, drained*

1 (12 oz.) jar artichoke hearts, drained and finely chopped

1 (10oz.) package chopped frozen spinach, thawed and drained

½ cup GF sour cream

½ cup GF mayonnaise

¾ cup shredded Monterey Jack cheese**

¼ teaspoon pepper

Preheat oven to 400°.  Mix all ingredients together, reserving ¼ cup of cheese for the topping.  Spread into a 9inch oven-proof casserole dish or pie plate.  Sprinkle with remaining cheese.  Bake for 20 minutes or until cheese is bubbling.

*Can substitute with 2 tablespoons pimentos, drained

**Can substitute with 1 cup of feta cheese

# Spinach Balls

2 (10oz.) packages frozen spinach, thawed and drained

½ cup onion, minced

½ cup parmesan cheese, shredded

1 cup cooked rice

3 eggs

2 tablespoons butter

1/8 teaspoon nutmeg (optional)

¼ teaspoon salt

¼ teaspoon pepper

Preheat oven to 350°. Melt 2 tablespoons of butter and let it cool slightly. Beat eggs in a medium bowl. Stir in onion, butter, spinach, rice, cheese, nutmeg, salt and pepper. Lightly grease or use GF cooking spray* to coat the bottom of a 13x9 inch baking pan. Form mixture into golf ball size servings, and place in pan without the balls touching. Bake for 20-25 minutes until lightly browned. Best served warm.

*Be careful which cooking spray you buy at the grocery store. Some brands have started adding flour to their spray.

# Bean Dip

1 tablespoon olive oil

1 (15.5oz.) can black beans, drained

1 (15.5oz.) can pinto beans, drained

½ medium onion, chopped

½ cup finely chopped roasted red pepper (optional)

1/3 cup fresh cilantro or parsley

1 clove garlic, minced

1 (4oz.) can green chiles, drained

Juice of 1 lemon or 2 limes

1 cup cheddar cheese

Preheat oven to 350°. In a skillet over medium heat, sauté oil, onion and garlic until tender, about 5 minutes. Add beans, red pepper, chiles and cilantro or parsley. Cook for 5 minutes, stirring frequently. Remove from heat and mash with a fork or potato masher. Stir in lemon or lime juice and cheese. Pour into an oven-save baking dish and bake for 10-15 minutes, or until cheese is melted.

# Soups

# Chili

1 pound ground beef or turkey

1 cup chopped onions

2 cloves garlic, minced

1 (28oz.) can diced tomatoes*

1 teaspoon salt

½ teaspoon pepper

1 tablespoon chili powder

1 (15oz.) can kidney beans

1 teaspoon cumin

1 green bell pepper, seeded and chopped

2 chili peppers, seeded and chopped (optional)

1 teaspoon hot pepper sauce (optional)

In a skillet over medium heat, sauté onion, garlic, and green pepper until tender. Remove from pan and set aside. In the same pan, brown the meat with the chili peppers and drain. In a large saucepan, combine tomatoes, chili powder, cumin, hot pepper sauce, salt and pepper. Bring to a boil and add meat and onion mix. Cook uncovered under low heat for 30 minutes. Stir in kidney beans with liquid and heat an additional 5 minutes.

*Some grocery stores also carry diced tomatoes with green chiles added. You may use this to substitute the chili peppers or to make a spicier chili.

# Manhattan Clam Chowder

2 (10oz) cans whole baby clams

2 slices GF bacon, chopped

1 cup chopped celery

1 cup chopped onion

1 (14.5 oz.) can diced tomatoes

1 cup diced potatoes

½ cup finely chopped carrot

1 clove garlic, minced

½ teaspoon thyme

½ teaspoon parsley

½ teaspoon pepper

¼ teaspoon salt

Drain clams, reserving liquid. Add enough water to clam juice to equal 2 cups. In a large saucepan over medium heat, brown bacon. Add celery, onion, garlic and green pepper. Cook until the celery is tender. Stir in clam liquid, potatoes, tomatoes with liquid, carrots, thyme and parsley. Cover and simmer over low-medium heat for 30 minutes until potatoes are tender. Mash potatoes lightly with potato masher to thicken sauce. Add clams and heat thoroughly. Season with salt and pepper.

# Broccoli and Cheese Soup

2 tablespoons butter

½ cup chopped celery (optional)

½ cup chopped onion

2 tablespoons corn starch

1 large bunch fresh broccoli or 1 (16oz.) bag frozen chopped broccoli

3 cups milk

1 cup mild or sharp cheddar cheese

1 cup GF chicken or vegetable broth

½ teaspoon salt

½ teaspoon pepper

Cook broccoli, drain and set aside. In a large saucepan over medium heat, melt butter and sauté celery and onion until lightly browned. Mix cornstarch with ½ cup milk and add to pan with remaining milk and broccoli. Simmer over low heat, stirring frequently, until sauce starts to thicken. Stir in cheese and heat thoroughly.

# Fish and Potato Chowder

1 pound fresh haddock, cut into pieces

4 cups milk

2 cups peeled and diced potatoes

2 tablespoons butter

1 clove garlic, minced

1 cup corn

¼ cup chopped onion

2 tablespoons fresh parsley or 2 teaspoons dried parsley

1 cup frozen peas (optional)

1 tablespoon lemon juice

½ teaspoon pepper

½ teaspoon salt

In a large saucepan over low-medium heat, combine milk, potatoes and salt. Heat, stirring occasionally for 30 minutes. Meanwhile in a skillet over medium heat, melt butter. Add onion and garlic and cook until onion is translucent. Set aside. When potatoes are done, remove 1 cup of potatoes and 1 cup of liquid. Blend together until smooth in a blender or with a potato masher. Put back in pan and add fish, onions, garlic, corn, peas, parsley, pepper and lemon juice. Bring to a boil, then reduce heat and simmer 10 minutes or until fish is cooked through.

# Chicken Soup

1 tablespoon olive oil

2 carrots, chopped

2 celery stalks, chopped

1 ½ cups chopped onion

1 clove garlic, minced

4 cups GF chicken broth

1 pound boneless, skinless chicken breast, cut into cubes

2 tablespoons lemon juice

2 cup cooked rice or favorite GF pasta

¼ teaspoon salt

½ teaspoon pepper

In a large pot over medium heat, brown chicken. Remove and set aside. In the same pot, add carrots, celery, onion, garlic, salt and pepper and sauté for 5 minutes over medium heat. Add broth and simmer 30-35 minutes over low-medium heat. During the last 15 minutes of cooking, add chicken, lemon juice and rice or pasta.

# Black Bean Soup

2 tablespoons olive oil

1 medium onion, chopped

2 cloves garlic, minced

1 teaspoon oregano

1 teaspoon cumin

1 (14.5 oz.) can diced tomatoes

¼ cup salsa (optional)

2 (15.5oz.) cans black beans, drained

1 (14.5oz.) can GF chicken broth

In a large saucepan over medium heat, cook oil, onion, garlic, oregano and cumin. Cook about 3-5 minutes, stirring often, until onion begins to brown. Add tomatoes, salsa, black beans and chicken broth. Bring to a boil, stirring occasionally. Puree soup in a blender or food processor (if a chunkier soup is preferred, use a potato masher). Return to pan and heat for 5-7 minutes over low-medium heat.

# Greens and Beans

3 bunches of escarole

1 ½ pounds GF medium or hot sausage

3 cloves garlic, minced

2 (15oz.) cans cannelini beans (white kidney beans), drained

½ cup olive oil

3 (14.5oz) GF chicken broth

2 cups water

½ teaspoon salt

½ teaspoon pepper

½ cup grated parmesan cheese

Chop escarole and rinse thoroughly in a colander.  In a large covered saucepan, add 2 cups of water and escarole.  Boil until escarole is tender and wilted.  Drain liquid and set escarole aside.  In saucepan, brown sausage.  Add olive oil and garlic and sauté for 5 minutes.  Add escarole, beans and broth.  Bring to a boil, cover and reduce heat to low for 30 minutes.  Sprinkle with cheese when serving.

# Side Dishes

# Risotto

1 cup rice (preferably Arborio rice)

¼ cup water*

1 ½ cups GF chicken or vegetable broth*

2 tablespoons butter

½ cup heavy cream

½ cup grated parmesan cheese

½ teaspoon salt

½ teaspoon pepper

Combine rice, water and GF chicken broth in a medium saucepan. Bring to a boil. Cook over medium-high heat until most of the liquid is absorbed, stirring constantly. Add butter, cover and simmer over low heat for five minutes. Stir in heavy cream and parmesan cheese. Continue stirring over low heat until cheese is melted, approximately five minutes. Serve immediately.

*Can substitute ¼ cup of water and 1 ½ cups GF chicken broth with 1 ¼ cups water and ½ cup white wine.

# Broccoli with Sesame Seeds

1 large bunch of fresh broccoli

2 tablespoons sesame seeds

3 tablespoons olive oil

2 cloves garlic, minced

¼ cup GF chicken stock

3 tablespoons GF soy sauce

½ teaspoon sugar

Cut broccoli into florets. In a preheated dry skillet or wok toast sesame seeds for 1-2 minutes, shaking constantly. Set aside. Heat oil in a skillet or wok over medium heat. Stir in garlic, chicken stock, soy sauce and sugar. Mix together for 1-2 minutes and add broccoli. Reduce heat to low and cover. Steam for 3-4 minutes or until broccoli is just tender. Transfer to a serving dish and sprinkle with sesame seeds.

# Cold Rice Salad

2 cups cooked rice, cooled
¼ cup chopped onion
½ cup diced red or green bell pepper
¼ cup diced celery
¼ cup sliced green olives, drained
¾ cup GF Italian dressing or vinaigrette
½ cup canned corn (optional)
¾ cup cherry tomatoes, halved (optional)

Combine all ingredients and refrigerate before serving.

# Sausage and Cornbread Stuffing

1 prepared GF cornbread recipe (page 120)*

1 tablespoon olive oil

1 pound GF sausage

2 celery stalks, chopped

1 carrot, chopped

2 shallots, finely chopped

1 onion, chopped

2 cloves garlic, minced

3 tablespoons fresh sage

1 tablespoon fresh parsley

1 tablespoon fresh thyme

2 cups GF chicken broth

¼ teaspoon salt

½ teaspoon pepper

Chop prepared cornbread into ½ inch cubes and leave uncovered on a baking sheet overnight to dry. You may also slowly dry in a 200° oven, checking often.

Preheat oven to 375°. Heat olive oil in a large skillet. Cook sausage and remove with a slotted spoon and set aside. In the same pan, add the celery, carrots, shallots, onion and garlic. Sauté until vegetables are translucent. Add the sage, parsley, thyme, salt and pepper and cook for one minute more. Add the chicken broth and bring to a boil. Remove from heat. In a large bowl, combine the dried cornbread, sausage and vegetable mixture. Place in a 13x9 inch baking dish and cover with foil. Bake for 25-30 minutes, remove foil and bake an additional 5 minutes.

If your stuffing is too dry, drizzle with more chicken stock, if it is too soggy, bake uncovered an additional 2-3 minutes.

You can also substitute your favorite GF bread.

# Greens

1 large head of escarole

1 cup water

4 thin slices of GF prosciutto or GF ham, chopped (optional)

2 cloves garlic, minced

2 tablespoons olive oil

2 Italian long hot hoppers or ½ cup cherry peppers*

½ cup GF breadcrumbs

½ cup grated parmesan cheese

1 cup GF chicken or vegetable broth

¼ cup diced onion

½ cup red or green bell pepper, chopped

Chop escarole into large pieces and clean thoroughly in a colander. In a medium saucepan, combine the water and escarole and boil under medium heat until the escarole is tender and wilted. Drain any excess water. Heat olive oil in a medium skillet. Add onion, garlic, bell peppers and prosciutto or ham. Cook 3-4 minutes and then add the hot peppers. Cook an additional 2-3 minutes. Stir in the chicken broth with ½ of the bread crumbs and cheese. Place in an 8x8 inch casserole dish and sprinkle with the remaining bread crumbs and cheese. Broil for 3-5 minutes.

*Can usually be found in the Italian section of most grocery stores.

# Grilled Zucchini with Parmesan Cheese

2 medium zucchini

¼ cup olive oil

2 tablespoons parmesan cheese

¼ teaspoon salt

½ teaspoon pepper

Preheat grill or oven broiler to low.  Cut zucchini in half, lengthwise.  Microwave on high for 5 minutes.  Drizzle each half with olive oil.  Sprinkle with parmesan cheese, salt and pepper.  Place halves back together and wrap with foil.  Grill for 15-20 minutes or broil for 10-15 minutes, turning once.

# Spanish Rice

1 pound ground beef

1 medium onion chopped

1 medium green bell pepper, chopped

2 (14.5 oz.) cans diced tomatoes

1 cup water

1 cup uncooked rice

½ teaspoon chili powder

¾ teaspoon oregano

½ teaspoon salt

½ teaspoon red pepper flakes

1 clove garlic, minced

In a large skillet, sauté beef, onion, green pepper and garlic until meat is browned. Drain and return to pan with remaining ingredients. Bring to a boil, cover and reduce heat to low-medium. Simmer 30 minutes or until rice is tender, stirring occasionally.

# *Fried Zucchini or Tomatoes*

3 large tomatoes or 2 medium zucchini (or both)

½ cup cornmeal

3 tablespoons olive oil

½ teaspoon salt

¼ teaspoon pepper

Slice tomatoes into ½ inch slices. Slice zucchini ¼ inch slices. Combine cornmeal, salt and pepper. Dip tomatoes or zucchini in cornmeal and shake off excess. Heat olive oil in a medium skillet and fry until browned on both sides, approximately 5 minutes.

# Green Bean Casserole

1 pound fresh green beans

½ cup sliced onion

2 tablespoons butter

8 oz. chopped mushrooms

½ clove garlic, minced

¾ cup GF chicken or vegetable broth

½ cup heavy cream

½ teaspoon salt

½ teaspoon pepper

In a large saucepan, add green beans, salt and enough water to just cover beans. Cover and cook over high heat for five minutes. Drain and drop beans into a bowl of ice water. Drain again and set aside. Melt butter in the same saucepan, adding mushrooms, garlic and pepper. Cook on medium, stirring constantly for 3-5 minutes. Add chicken stock and heavy cream. Simmer over low heat until sauce thickens, about 10-15 minutes.

Preheat oven to 425° Sauté onions in a small skillet until brown and caramelized. Mix green beans and sauce and pour into a casserole dish. Top with onions and cover with foil. Bake 10-15 minutes.

Mushroom cream sauce is also good served over chicken or rice.

# Onion Bake

1 pound onions (preferably Vidalia if available)

3 tablespoons butter

2 eggs

½ cup milk

½ teaspoon salt

½ teaspoon pepper

Preheat oven to 400°. Peel onion and slice as thin as possible (a food processor works well). Melt butter in a medium skillet over medium heat. Add onions and cook until soft and translucent, about 10 minutes. Cool the onions slightly. Whisk the eggs, milk and salt in a separate bowl. Mix with onions and pour into an oven-safe casserole dish. Top with pepper and bake 15-20 minutes. Cool for 5 minutes before serving.

# Tuna Stuffed Tomatoes

3-4 medium sized tomatoes

¼ cup chopped celery

3 tablespoons GF mayonnaise or plain yogurt

2 tablespoons chopped onion

¼ teaspoon dill weed

1 (6oz.) can tuna, drained

Cut a small slice from the top of tomatoes. Scoop out the core and seeds and invert on a paper towel to drain. Mix all remaining ingredients together and fill tomatoes. Refrigerate until ready to be served.

# Mushroom Stuffed Tomatoes

5-6 medium tomatoes

¾ cup fresh mushrooms, finely chopped

4 tablespoons butter

4 tablespoons minced onion

1 (3oz.) package cream cheese

¾ cup GF sour cream or ¾ cup plain yogurt

3 tablespoons fresh dill

Cut a small slice from the top of tomatoes. Scoop out the core and seeds and invert on a paper towel to drain. Sauté onions and mushrooms with butter in a skillet over medium heat until lightly browned. Whip sour cream or yogurt with cream cheese in a bowl until smooth. Mix with slightly cooled mushroom mix. Stuff the tomatoes and top will dill. Refrigerate until ready to be served.

# Herb Sausage

1 pound ground pork or turkey

¼ cup fresh parsley or 1 tablespoon dried parsley

2 tablespoons fresh thyme or 2 teaspoons dried thyme

1 tablespoon fresh sage or 1 teaspoon dried sage

1 teaspoon salt

½ teaspoon pepper

4 scallions, finely chopped or ½ cup chopped onion

1 tablespoon olive oil

2 teaspoons red pepper flakes (optional)

Mix all ingredients except oil in a large boil until well-combined. Heat oil in a large skillet over medium-high heat cook until sausage is browned. Drain excess liquid.

You can also form the mixture into about 18 balls and flatten to make sausage patties. This recipe also works well for homemade gluten-free sausage bread.

# Rice Pilaf

3 tablespoons butter

¼ cup minced onions

1 clove garlic, minced

1½ cups rice

3 cups GF chicken or vegetable broth

1 (4 oz.) can sliced mushrooms, drained

½ cup chopped celery (optional)

½ teaspoon salt

½ teaspoon pepper

Melt butter in a large skillet over medium heat.  Add onion, garlic, celery, mushroom, and pepper, cooking about 5 minutes.  Stir in rice and chicken broth.  Bring to a boil, cover and simmer over low heat until most of the liquid is absorbed and the rice is fluffy, about 20 minutes.  Remove from heat and let stand 5 minutes before serving.

# Cole Slaw

4 cups shredded cabbage

½ cup finely chopped celery

¼ cup shredded carrot

¼ cup finely chopped onion

1/3 cup GF mayonnaise

2 tablespoons GF vinegar

½ teaspoon sugar

1/8 teaspoon salt

½ teaspoon pepper

Mix together cabbage, celery, carrot and onion.  In a separate bowl, combine mayonnaise, vinegar, sugar, salt and pepper.  Pour over cabbage mixture and mix well.  Cover and chill 2-3 hours before serving.

# Hush Puppies

2 cups cornmeal

½ cup GF flour

2 teaspoons GF baking powder

2 teaspoons salt

2 eggs

2 tablespoons minced onion

2/3 cup buttermilk*

1 tablespoon sugar

Mix together cornmeal, flour, baking powder, and salt.  In a separate bowl, beat egg, onion and buttermilk.  Pour into cornmeal mixture and stir together until just moistened.  The mixture should hold its shape with a spoon.  Heat oil in a deep skillet or deep fryer until it is about 350°.  Drop carefully by spoonfuls and fry about 2 minutes until evenly browned.

*Can substitute 2/3 cup buttermilk by whisking together 1 teaspoon lemon juice with plain milk.

# Glazed Carrots

1 pound carrots

¾ cup water

3 tablespoons butter

1 tablespoon brown sugar

1 teaspoon thyme

1 teaspoon rosemary

1 teaspoon salt

½ teaspoon pepper

Preheat oven to 350°. Cut carrots into sticks (or use baby carrots). Cover with water and salt in a medium saucepan and bring to a boil. Cook over medium heat for about 5 minutes, until just tender. Drain. Melt butter and combine with brown sugar, thyme, rosemary and pepper. Toss butter with carrots and pour into an oven-safe baking dish. Bake uncovered for 10 minutes, serving immediately.

# Baked Fennel

2 large heads fennel

¼ cup butter, softened

1 teaspoon salt

½ teaspoon pepper

When purchasing fresh fennel, the bulb should be white or pale green in color, while the stalks and leaves should be green in color. It should also smell a little bit like licorice.

Preheat oven to 375°. Wash, trim off the stalks and leaves and cut the bulbs in half. Spread each half with butter and sprinkle with salt and pepper, put the bulbs back together and wrap in foil. Bake for 45 minutes or until tender.

# Marinated Mushrooms

1 pound small, whole mushrooms

½ cup olive oil

2 tablespoons lemon juice

2 tablespoons red wine vinegar

1 teaspoon salt

½ teaspoon pepper

¼ teaspoon thyme

1 teaspoon tarragon

1 clove garlic, minced

Clean and dry mushrooms using a soft brush or damp paper towel. Combine mushrooms, olive oil, lemon juice, vinegar, salt pepper, thyme, tarragon and garlic in a medium saucepan. Simmer covered over low heat for 10 minutes. Cool and refrigerate overnight. Serve at room temperature.

# Hash Browns

2 large baking potatoes

2 tablespoons chopped onion

1 clove garlic, minced

½ teaspoon salt

½ teaspoon pepper

¼ teaspoon thyme

In a large pot with water, boil peeled potatoes until just tender. Or, poke potatoes with a fork and cook in microwave on high for 5-8 minutes. (This is also a great way to use leftover baked potatoes.) When cooled, shred potatoes and combine with onion, garlic, salt, pepper and thyme. Coat a medium skillet with GF cooking spray and heat over medium-high heat. Form mix into patties about 2 inches wide. Cook for 5-7 minutes on each side until browned.

# Mexican Corn

2 cups fresh corn (about 4 ears of corn)

2 tablespoons butter

1 medium onion, chopped

1/3 cup chopped green bell pepper

1/3 cup chopped red bell pepper

¼ teaspoon oregano

¼ teaspoon red pepper flakes

1 medium tomato, diced

½ teaspoon salt

½ teaspoon pepper

Remove the corn from the cob and mix with the onion, peppers, oregano and red pepper flakes. In a medium skillet, melt butter over medium heat. Add corn mixture and cook approximately 10 minutes until corn is tender, stirring occasionally. Stir in diced tomatoes and cook another 2 minutes. Serve warm or cold.

# Tomato and Cucumber Salad

3 large tomatoes, chopped

2 large cucumbers, chopped

1 medium onion, diced

2 tablespoons fresh dill or 2 teaspoons dried dill

½ cup favorite GF salad dressing or vinaigrette

This recipe can be made anytime, but is best during the summer when all ingredients are the freshest. Chop vegetables into bite-size pieces. Mix with dill and dressing and refrigerate.

# Rice Dressing/Stuffing

3 cups cooked rice

1 small onion, finely chopped

½ cup sliced mushrooms

½ cup chopped celery

1 (8oz.) can water chestnuts, drained and coarsely chopped

¼ cup butter

½ teaspoon salt

¼ teaspoon pepper

1 teaspoon thyme

½ teaspoon rosemary

½ teaspoon sage

½ teaspoon parsley

1 clove garlic, minced

Melt butter in a medium saucepan over medium heat. Sauté onion, mushrooms, celery, water chestnuts and garlic for about 5 minutes. Add rice and seasonings and heat thoroughly. This recipe is enough to stuff a 10 lb. turkey or serve as a side dish.

# *Meatballs*

2 pounds ground beef or turkey

1 cup GF bread crumbs or GF corn flake crumbs

½ cup grated parmesan cheese

2 cloves garlic, minced

3 eggs

¼ cup fresh parsley, minced

½ teaspoon salt

½ teaspoon pepper

½ cup milk or tomato sauce

Preheat oven to 350°. Combine all ingredients in a large bowl, mixing together thoroughly. Roll into 2 inch round meatballs. Add ¼ cup of water to the bottom of a rimmed baking sheet or casserole dish (to help keep meatballs from sticking). Bake for 20-25 minutes, turning once.

*"All people are made alike-*
*of bones and flesh and dinner-*
*Only the dinners are different."*

~Gertrude Louise Cheney

# Main Dishes

# Stuffed Eggplant

1 eggplant

2 tablespoons olive oil

1 can (6oz) tomato puree

1 small onion, chopped

1 clove garlic, minced

½ pound ground meat (beef, chicken or turkey)*

1 cup cooked rice

1 tablespoon parsley

½ cup shredded mozzarella cheese

¼ cup feta cheese (optional)

½ (10oz.) package frozen chopped spinach, thawed and drained

½ teaspoon salt

½ teaspoon pepper

Remove the stem from the eggplant and cut in half lengthwise. Boil in salted water until tender (about 10 minutes.) Drain and let cool slightly. Scoop out the inside of the eggplant and coarsely chop.

Preheat oven to 350°. In a large skillet, heat oil and add onion, garlic and meat. Sauté until meat is browned. Remove from heat and drain excess liquid. Stir in rice, eggplant, feta cheese, parsley, spinach, salt and pepper. Sprinkle with mozzarella cheese. Bake covered in a baking dish for 45 minutes, uncovered for last 10 minutes.

*Can substitute with 8oz. firm tofu.

# *Veggie Paella*

2 tablespoons olive oil

1 onion, thinly sliced

1 clove garlic, minced

1 red bell pepper, diced

2 cups uncooked rice

2 cups GF chicken or vegetable broth

2 medium tomatoes, chopped and seeded

½ cup fresh green beans or frozen green beans, thawed

2 celery stalks, chopped

½ cup black olives, sliced (optional)

½ teaspoon salt

½ teaspoon pepper

Heat oil in a large skillet over medium heat. Sauté onion, garlic and green pepper. Cook until onions are translucent, about 5 minutes. Stir in rice, cooking another 2-3 minutes. Pour in broth and increase heat to high. Bring to a boil, stir in tomatoes, green beans, celery, black olives, salt and pepper. Reduce heat to low, cover and simmer for 30-35 minutes until rice is tender.

# Greek Rice Pizza

*Pizza Crust:*
3 cups cooked rice, cooled slightly*
2 eggs, beaten
1 cup shredded mozzarella cheese
1/8 cup GF flour or cornmeal for dusting

*Pizza Toppings:*
1 small onion, thinly sliced
5-6 artichoke hearts, chopped
¼ cup crumbled feta cheese
¼ cup sun dried tomatoes
¼ cup black or kalamata olives
½ cup sliced mushrooms
½ cup shredded mozzarella cheese
½ tablespoon oregano

*To make the crust:* Preheat oven to 425°. Mix all ingredients well. Spread evenly and press onto a baking sheet dusted with GF flour or cornmeal. This recipe makes two 12 inch crusts or four 6 inch crusts. Bake for 15 minutes. Can top with your favorite sauce and ingredients or freeze between layers of wax/parchment paper.

*To make the pizza:* Add your choice of toppings and return to 400° oven to melt cheeses and/or unthaw crust.

*You can also replace 1 cup of cooked rice with 1 cup of zucchini. Peel, shred and dry the zucchini with paper towel before adding to mixture.

# Spinach and Ricotta Pasta

1 (8oz.) package GF pasta

1 (10oz.) package frozen chopped spinach, thawed and drained

2 tablespoons olive oil

2 tablespoons butter

1 clove garlic, minced

1 teaspoon parsley

1 teaspoon oregano

½ cup grated parmesan cheese

1 cup ricotta cheese

Cook pasta according to package directions (penne pasta works well for this recipe). In a medium skillet, sauté olive oil, butter and garlic over medium heat. Add cheeses, parsley, oregano and cooked pasta to pan. Heat thoroughly. Serve immediately.

# Scallop and Vegetable Kabobs

1 pound sea scallops

12 GF bacon strips, cut in half

2 cups whole mushrooms

1 large red or green bell pepper, cut into 1 inch pieces

1 medium onion, cut into 1 inch chunks

2 cups whole cherry tomatoes

1 cup GF marinade (recipes page 97)

Bamboo skewers

Soak skewers in water for 30 minutes.  Wrap each scallop in bacon and thread onto skewers (will fill about 4 skewers).  On separate skewers, place other vegetables.  Brush with marinade and refrigerate for 1 hour to overnight.  Broil or cook on barbeque grill until bacon is crisp and vegetable are tender.  Keep scallops and vegetable on separate skewers, as the scallops will cook faster than the vegetables.

# Artichoke Quiche

1 (12oz.) jar artichoke hearts, drained

¼ cup fresh mushrooms, sliced

1 tablespoon butter

2 cups shredded parmesan, swiss or cheddar cheese (or a mix)

4 eggs, beaten

1 cup milk

½ cup chopped onion

½ teaspoon pepper

¼ teaspoon basil

Preheat oven to 350°. Spray a 9 inch pie plate or quiche dish with GF cooking spray. Roughly chop artichokes and place in bottom of dish. In a small skillet, sauté mushrooms and onions in butter until onions are translucent. Pour over artichokes. Sprinkle with shredded cheese. In a separate bowl, whisk together eggs, milk, pepper and basil. Pour into pie plate. Bake 30-40 minutes or until the center of quiche is firm.

# Stuffed Peppers

4 medium green bell peppers
1 tablespoon olive oil
2 cups cooked rice
1 clove garlic, minced
1 pound ground beef or turkey
1 can (14.5oz.) tomato sauce
½ teaspoon salt
½ teaspoon pepper

Clean peppers, remove stem, core and seeds. Place in boiling water for 10 minutes, remove and drain peppers. Preheat oven to 350°.

In a medium skillet, sauté olive oil and garlic for 2-3 minutes over medium heat. Add beef and cook until browned. Mix in ¼ cup tomatoes, rice, salt and pepper. Using all of the mixture, stuff the peppers and place in a shallow baking dish. Pour the remaining tomatoes around the peppers. Bake for 25 minutes. Spoon tomato sauce over peppers and serve hot.

# Stuffed Chicken Breasts

Preheat oven to 350°. Place boneless, skinless chicken breasts between 2 sheets of plastic wrap or wax paper. Pound until flattened to about ¼ inch thick. Fill with your favorite ingredients, roll up and secure with a toothpick. Bake for 30-35 minutes. The following ingredients are the amounts for each piece of chicken.

*Chicken Cordon Bleu:* 1 slice of GF ham and one slice of swiss cheese. Dip in ¼ cup GF breadcrumbs or GF corn flake crumbs

*Spinach & Cheese:* 2 tablespoons fresh baby spinach or thawed and drained chopped spinach mixed with 1 tablespoon crumbled feta or ricotta cheese

*Salsa & Cheddar:* 1 tablespoon GF salsa (pages 17 and 24) and 2 tablespoons grated cheddar cheese

*Chicken and Greens:* 2 tablespoons greens (page 46)

*Chicken and stuffing:* 2 tablespoons cornbread or rice stuffing (pages 45 and 64)

*Feta, mushroom and tomato:* 1 tablespoon crumbled feta cheese mix with 1 tablespoon chopped mushrooms and ½ tablespoon sun-dried tomatoes

*Apples and cheddar:* 1 tablespoon finely chopped apple mixed with 1 tablespoon shredded cheddar cheese

*Other ideas for leftover gluten-free stuffed chicken:* Olive Tapenade (page 16), Roasted Red Pepper Dip (page 19), Spicy Olive Dip (page 23), Broccoli and Sesame Seeds (page 43), Spanish Rice (page 48), Herb Sausage (page 54)

# Spaghetti Pie

1 (8oz.) package GF spaghetti

1 egg, beaten

1 tablespoon butter, melted

1/3 cup grated parmesan cheese

1 cup ricotta cheese

½ pound cooked meat (beef, sausage, turkey or sliced meatballs)

1 cup prepared GF spaghetti sauce

½ cup shredded mozzarella cheese

Spray a 9 inch pie plate with GF cooking spray. Cook spaghetti following package instructions and drain.

Preheat oven to 350°. In a large bowl, combine the egg, parmesan cheese and butter. Add pasta and mix until evenly coated. Add spaghetti to pie plate, pressing to form a crust (optional-reserve ½ cup pasta for the top of the pie). Spread ricotta cheese over spaghetti. Mix spaghetti sauce with meat and pour over ricotta cheese. Sprinkle with mozzarella cheese. (Optional-arrange the reserved spaghetti on top of the dish to look like a lattice pie crust). Bake for 30-35 minutes. Remove foil for the last 10 minutes of baking. Cut into pie-shaped slices.

# Cinnamon French Toast

8 slices GF bread

2 eggs

1 teaspoon sugar

½ teaspoon cinnamon*

1 teaspoon GF vanilla extract

1/8 teaspoon nutmeg (optional)

2 tablespoons vegetable oil or GF cooking spray

1 tablespoon cinnamon/sugar mix

Whisk together eggs, sugar, cinnamon, vanilla and nutmeg.  Heat oil or GF cooking spray in a large skillet or griddle over medium-high heat.  Dip bread in egg mixture until well coated.  Cook on skillet, turning when slightly brown and sprinkle with cinnamon sugar.

If using GF cinnamon bread, lesson or omit the amount of cinnamon added.

# Cornmeal Blueberry Pancakes

2 cups buttermilk*

1 ½ cups cornmeal

1 cup GF flour

½ teaspoon xanthan gum

2 tablespoons sugar

2 teaspoons GF baking powder

½ teaspoon salt

1 egg

3 tablespoons butter, melted and room temp.

1 tablespoon vegetable oil or GF cooking spray

1 cup fresh or frozen blueberries*

Mix together cornmeal, flour, xanthan gum, baking powder, sugar and salt in a medium bowl.  In a separate bowl, whisk together the egg, butter and milk.  Make well in the center of the dry ingredients and pour the milk mixture into the center. Gently mix until just combined, and a few lumps remain.  Heat a non-stick skillet or griddle on medium for 3-5 minutes.  Add oil or remove from heat and spray with GF cooking spray.  Pour ¼ cup batter onto skillet, sprinkle with blueberries and cook until bubbles begin to appear on the pancakes.  Flip and finish cooking.

Serve with maple syrup or fruit sauce recipes (pages 106-108)  Makes 14- 4inch pancakes.  You can freeze the extra pancakes (not the batter) and put into the toaster one at a time.

*Can substitute with 2 cups plain milk whisked with 1 tablespoon lemon juice

# Easy Omelets

Quart-Size plastic freezer bags (must be freezer bags!)

2 eggs per person

*Omelet ingredients including:*

Cheeses, onions, pepper, ham, mushrooms, salsa, spinach, bacon, sausage and broccoli

Fill a large stock pot ¾ full with water.  Bring to a boil.  Crack 2 eggs into each bag and write each person's name with permanent marker on the outside of the bag.  Let each person add their own ingredients and shake to combine.  Close the bag securely, removing all of the air out of the bag.  Place bags into boiling water and time for exactly 13 minutes.  Depending on the size of you pot, you should be able to fit 6-8 omelets, so that all the omelets are done at the same time.  Remove from bag carefully, by sliding the omelet out onto the plate.

*This recipe has been around for quite awhile, but it works well for people with celiac disease, since there is no cross-contamination of ingredients in a skillet.*

# Spinach Gnocchi

1 cup chopped frozen spinach, defrosted and drained

1 cup ricotta cheese

1/3 cup grated parmesan cheese

1 egg, lightly beaten

2 tablespoons butter

½ teaspoon salt

¼ teaspoon pepper

¼ teaspoon nutmeg (optional)

½ cup GF flour

2 tablespoons butter

Preheat oven to 400° and start a medium saucepan boiling 4 cups of water. Mix spinach with ricotta, ½ of the parmesan cheese, salt, pepper and nutmeg. Add the egg, beating until the mix holds its shape. Using a small amount of GF flour in your hands, shape 1 tablespoon of mix into an egg shape. In a saucepan with boiling water, gently drop 3 or 4 at a time, cooking 1-2 minutes each. Remove with a slotted spoon and place into a lightly sprayed casserole dish. Sprinkle with parmesan cheese and dot with butter. Bake for 10 minutes and serve immediately. Serve with your favorite pasta sauce or topping.

# Corn Dogs

¾ cup milk

2 eggs

¼ cup vegetable oil

2 tablespoons sugar or honey

1 teaspoon GF baking powder

1 1/3 cup cornmeal

2/3 cup GF flour

1/8 teaspoon xanthan gum

1 ½ pounds GF hot dogs

4 tablespoons corn starch

½ teaspoon salt

Oil for deep drying

Popsicle sticks

In a large bowl, whisk together milk, eggs, oil, sugar or honey and salt. Stir in baking powder, cornmeal, GF flour and xanthan gum until just combined. There should still be some lumps.

Heat oil in a deep skillet or deep fryer to at least 375° (if oil isn't hot enough, the batter will slide off the hot dogs). Dry hot dogs well. Dust with corn starch. Pour batter into a glass or tall skinny jar. Put hot dogs on a popsicle stick (or cut in half, to make it easier) and dip into jar to cover the hot dog with cornmeal mix. Quickly dip into hot oil and cook until browned, turning once. Remove with tongs and drain on paper towels.

Unfortunately, oven-baking these corn dogs doesn't work well, but they can be frozen ahead of time and reheated on a cookie sheet at 350°.

# Eggplant Roll-ups

2 medium eggplants

1 egg, beaten

½ cup GF flour

2 tablespoons olive oil

1 cup shredded mozzarella cheese

1 (15oz.) container ricotta cheese

1 tablespoon fresh basil

2 cups GF tomato sauce


Preheat oven to 350°. Remove the stems from the eggplants, peel and slice lengthwise into ¼ inch slices. Dip in egg, shake off excess and dip in flour to coat. Heat olive oil in a medium skillet over medium-high heat. Fry each slice of eggplant until lightly browned. Place on sheet of paper towels to drain and cool slightly. Mix together ricotta, mozzarella and basil and spread over each slice of eggplant. Roll up each slice and place in an oven-safe casserole dish so that they are tightly packed together in a single layer. Pour tomato sauce over the top and bake for 15-20 minutes.

# Meatloaf

1 pound ground beef or turkey

½ cup finely chopped onion

¼ cup finely chopped celery

3 tablespoons fresh parsley

1 clove garlic, minced

¾ cup GF bread crumbs or GF corn flake crumbs

¾ cup canned crushed tomatoes

1 egg, beaten

½ teaspoon salt

½ teaspoon pepper

½ teaspoon sage

Preheat oven to 350°. In a large bowl, blend all ingredients thoroughly. Press into a loaf pan and bake for 1 hour and 15 minutes.

# Shrimp Stir-Fry

¾ pound fresh or frozen shrimp, thawed

½ (16oz.) package frozen broccoli, thawed

1 (4oz.) can sliced mushrooms, drained

1 (8oz.) can water chestnuts, drained

1 medium onion, sliced

1 glove garlic, minced

2 teaspoons corn starch

2 tablespoons cold water

1 tablespoon olive oil or fish oil

3 tablespoons GF soy sauce

1/8 teaspoon ginger (optional)

2 cups cooked rice

Mix together water and cornstarch in a small bowl. Stir in sugar, salt, soy sauce and ginger. Prepare all other ingredients before heating oil in a wok or large skillet over medium-high heat. Cook water chestnuts, mushrooms, onion and garlic until onions are tender. Remove from heat and set aside. Add broccoli to pan and cook for 2-3 minutes, add shrimp and cook an additional 3-4 minutes. Return all vegetables and sauce and heat until sauce thickens. Serve over rice.

Variations: substitute scallops or tofu for shrimp; peas or sliced celery for broccoli; and bamboo shoots for water chestnuts

# Spaghetti Squash Bake

1 spaghetti squash

1 (14.5 oz.) can diced tomatoes

1 medium onion, finely chopped

1 teaspoon oregano

1 teaspoon basil

½ teaspoon salt

½ teaspoon pepper

2 tablespoons grated parmesan cheese

½ cup mozzarella cheese

Cut squash in half lengthwise and remove the seeds. Place squash cut sides up in a microwave-safe dish with ¼ cup of water. Cover with plastic wrap and cook on high for 10-12 minutes, depending on the size of the squash. Let stand covered for five minutes and scrape out inside with a fork into a large bowl.

Preheat oven to 350°. Mix together squash, tomatoes, onion, oregano, basil, salt and pepper. Pour into oven-safe casserole dish and sprinkle with parmesan and mozzarella cheeses. Bake covered for 30 minutes, uncovering for last 5 minutes.

# Spicy Chicken Nuggets

1 pound boneless, skinless chicken breasts or chicken tenders

½ cup cornmeal

1 teaspoon chili powder

1 teaspoon red pepper flakes

2 teaspoons GF hot sauce (optional)

1 egg

Preheat oven to 400°. Cut chicken into 1 inch pieces. In a plastic storage bag, combine the cornmeal, chili powder, and red pepper flakes. Whisk together the egg and hot sauce. Dip each piece of chicken into the egg mixture and drop into plastic bag. Close the bag tightly and shake to evenly coat the chicken. Place on a single layer on a baking sheet and bake for 8-10 minutes, turning once. Serve with your favorite GF dipping sauces.

# *Veggie Frittata*

½ cup chopped onion

1 clove garlic, minced

2 tablespoons butter

1 green or red bell pepper, chopped

¼ teaspoon salt

¼ teaspoon pepper

1 small tomato, chopped and seeded

2 small zucchini, sliced

6 eggs, beaten

¼ cup grated parmesan cheese

Preheat oven to 375°. In a small skillet over medium heat, melt butter and sauté onion and garlic until translucent. Add pepper and cook an additional 2 minutes. Add tomato, salt, pepper and zucchini and cook an additional 5 minutes, stirring occasionally. Transfer vegetables to an oven-safe casserole dish. Beat eggs in a separate bowl and pour over vegetables. Bake uncovered for 10-12 minutes, or until set. Sprinkle with cheese and serve immediately.

# Zucchini Lasagna

4 large zucchini (about 2 pounds)

1 large onion, sliced

½ pound sweet or hot GF sausage*

1 cup shredded mozzarella cheese

1 teaspoon salt

½ teaspoon pepper

1 teaspoon oregano

1 clove garlic, minced

1 can (14oz.) tomato puree

½ cup ricotta cheese

Preheat oven to 350°. Trim ends off zucchini and cut into thin lengthwise slices (like lasagna noodles). In a large skillet over medium-high heat, sauté the onion, garlic and sausage until the sausage is lightly browned. Remove from heat and mix with the salt, pepper, oregano and tomatoes. Place a small amount of tomato mixture on the bottom of a casserole dish. Layer 1/3 of the zucchini slices across the bottom of the dish. Add 1/3 of the mozzarella and ricotta cheeses. Add 1/3 of the tomato mixture. Finish layering in the following order: zucchini, ricotta and mozzarella, tomato mix, zucchini, ricotta, tomato mix and top with mozzarella cheese. Cover with foil and bake for 1 hour, or until the zucchini is tender. Remove the foil for the last 20 minutes of baking. Let stand for 15-20 minutes before slicing.

# *Chicken Riggies*

1 pound GF rigatoni

2 pounds boneless, skinless chicken breasts*

3 tablespoons olive oil

½ (4oz.) jar hot cherry peppers

½ cup GF tomato sauce

2 shallots, finely chopped**

1 small onion, chopped

1 green bell pepper, chopped

1 cup heavy cream***

1 cup fresh mushrooms, sliced

½ cup sliced black olives

½ teaspoon salt

¼ teaspoon pepper

Cook the GF pasta according to the directions on the package. In a large skillet over medium-high heat, sauté the oil, shallots and onion until the onions are translucent. Add the chicken and cook until lightly browned. Add peppers, tomato sauce, mushrooms, olives, salt and pepper. Simmer over low heat for 10 minutes. Stir in the cream and simmer another 10 minutes. Toss with GF pasta and serve immediately.

*Can substitute 2 pounds of shrimp for chicken, by adding with the tomato sauce, mushrooms and olives.

**Can substitute with 1 clove garlic, minced.

***Can substitute with ¾ cup GF chicken broth added with the tomato sauce, mushrooms, and olives.

# Shrimp Scampi

1 (8oz.) package GF linguine or spaghetti

1 pound fresh or frozen, thawed shrimp

4 tablespoons butter

2 tablespoons olive oil

1 clove garlic, minced

1 tablespoon chopped fresh parsley

¼ teaspoon pepper

1 tablespoon lemon juice

¼ cup grated parmesan cheese

Cook the GF pasta according to package directions. In a large skillet, sauté the butter, olive oil, and garlic over medium-low heat until the garlic is lightly browned. Add the shrimp in a single layer, cooking about 2 minutes on each side. Stir in the parsley and lemon juice and stir to coat. Remove from heat and toss with the GF pasta. Top with pepper and parmesan cheese.

# Spinach Quiche

1 (10oz.) package frozen chopped spinach, thawed and drained
½ pound swiss cheese, diced
3 eggs
1 cup milk
½ teaspoon salt
1/8 teaspoon pepper

Preheat oven to 350°. In a medium bowl, whisk together eggs, milk, salt and pepper. Stir in spinach and cheese until well blended. Spray a 9 inch pie plate with GF cooking spray. Pour mixture into pan and bake for 55-60 minutes, or until set. Let stand for 5-10 minutes.

# *Crispy Fried Scallops*

1 pound sea scallops, fresh or thawed

½ cup cornmeal

½ teaspoon salt

¼ teaspoon pepper

1 tablespoon lemon juice

3 tablespoons olive oil

Clean and dry scallops. Drizzle with lemon juice. In a medium bowl or plastic bag, mix together the cornmeal, salt and pepper. Dip scallops into mixture and shake off the excess. In a large skillet, heat the oil over medium heat. Add the scallops in a single layer, turning after 3-4 minutes. Cook until golden brown, being careful not to overcook. Drain on paper towels and serve immediately.

# Chicken Cacciatore

1 (8 oz.) package GF spaghetti or pasta

1 pound boneless, skinless chicken breasts, cut into 1inch pieces

2 tablespoons olive oil

1 clove garlic, minced

1 (28oz.) can diced tomatoes

1 (6oz.) can tomato puree

1 small onion, chopped

1 (4 oz.) can sliced mushrooms

1 can (14.5oz.) GF chicken broth

1 green bell pepper, diced

2 teaspoons parsley

1 teaspoon basil

1 teaspoon oregano

Cook the GF pasta according to package directions. In a large skillet over medium heat, cook the chicken with the olive oil until browned. In a large saucepan, sauté the olive oil, garlic, mushrooms, pepper and onion for about 3-5 minutes. Stir in the tomatoes, tomato puree, parsley, basil, oregano and chicken broth. Bring to a boil, cover, and reduce heat to low. Simmer for 45 minutes. Add the cooked chicken and simmer for another 15-20 minutes until sauce is thickened. Serve over GF spaghetti or pasta.

# Portabella Pizza

4 portabella mushrooms

2 tablespoons olive oil

¼ cup thinly sliced onions

2 Roma tomatoes, diced and seeded

1 clove garlic, minced

1 cup shredded mozzarella or crumbled feta cheese

3 tablespoons chopped basil leaves

Preheat oven to 350°. Clean mushrooms with a soft brush or damp paper towel and remove stems. Brush mushroom caps with 1 tablespoon olive oil. If mushrooms are larger than 4 inches in diameter, partially cook them in the oven for 3-4 minutes. In a medium skillet, sauté the olive oil, garlic, tomatoes and onion for 3-5 minutes. Top each mushroom with the mixture and sprinkle with basil and cheese. Bake for 3-6 minutes or until the cheese is melted.

You can also cook the portabella mushrooms on a barbeque grill over medium heat for 6-7 minutes.

Add any of your favorite toppings, including artichoke hearts, hot peppers, roasted red peppers, spinach, olives or GF pepperoni.

# Linguine and Red Clam Sauce

1 (8oz.) package GF linguine

2 tablespoons olive oil

1 (28oz.) can crushed tomatoes

1 (28oz.) can tomato puree

½ cup water

½ tablespoon parsley

½ tablespoon basil

¼ cup grated parmesan cheese

1 (8 oz.) bottle clam juice

2 (10 oz.) cans whole baby clams, rinsed and drained

½ teaspoon salt

¼ teaspoon pepper

Prepare linguine according to package directions. In a medium saucepan over medium heat, sauté oil and garlic until garlic just begins to brown. Add the tomatoes, tomato puree, water, parsley, basil, salt, pepper, clam juice and clams. Simmer over low heat for 15-20 minutes. Serve over linguine and top with parmesan cheese.

*"Let thy food be thy medicine and thy medicine by thy food."*

~*Hippocrates*

# Sauces and Marinades

# Hot Barbeque Marinade

1 cup Coca-Cola (not diet)
2 jalepeño peppers
1 clove garlic, minced
2 tablespoons brown sugar

Carefully remove the seeds and finely chop the jalepeño peppers.  Whisk all ingredients together in a medium bowl.  Cover chicken with marinade and refrigerate for 4 hours or overnight.  Discard any leftover marinade.

# Tequila Citrus Marinade

Juice and grated peel of 1 lime

Juice and grated peel of 1 lemon

¼ cup tequila

3 tablespoon olive oil

½ teaspoon pepper

¼ cup chopped fresh cilantro or parsley

Whisk all ingredients together and pour over chicken, pork, seafood, beef or vegetables. Keep in the refrigerator for four hours or overnight. Discard any leftover marinade.

# Orange Ginger Marinade

½ cup orange juice

3 tablespoons GF soy sauce

1 clove garlic, minced

½ teaspoon ginger

2 tablespoons olive oil

¼ teaspoon pepper

¼ teaspoon salt

Whisk all ingredients together and pour over chicken, pork, seafood, beef or vegetables. Keep in the refrigerator for four hours or overnight. Discard any leftover marinade.

# Pesto Sauce

2 cups fresh basil leaves

½ cup grated parmesan cheese

2 cloves garlic, minced

¼ cup toasted pine nuts (optional)

3 tablespoons olive oil

1 cup heavy cream (optional)

¼ teaspoon salt

½ teaspoon pepper

In a blender or food processor, combine the basil, cheese, garlic and pine nuts until well processed. Slowly add the olive and blend 15-30 seconds more. Transfer to a small saucepan and heat through over low-medium heat.

For a cream sauce, whisk in the heavy cream. Heat for 4-5 minutes, remove from heat and stir until sauce thickens.

# Green Sauce

1 (4oz.) can green chiles, drained
¼ cup chopped cilantro or parsley
Juice and zest of 1 lime
¼ cup chopped green onions or scallions
2 tablespoons olive oil

Whisk all ingredients together and heat over low-medium heat in a small saucepan. Good served over grilled chicken or seafood.

# Roasted Red Pepper Sauce

4 roasted red peppers

1 tablespoon fresh parsley

½ cup heavy cream

½ teaspoon salt

¼ teaspoon pepper

1 teaspoon red pepper flakes or red pepper sauce (optional)

Puree peppers in a food processor or blender.  Transfer to a bowl and set aside for 30 minutes.  The liquid will settle to the bottom of the bowl and the pulp will rise to the top.  In a small saucepan over low-medium heat, mix together the red pepper pulp, cream, parsley, salt, pepper and hot pepper.  Serve over pasta, meats or seafood.

# Barbeque Sauce

½ cup GF ketchup

¼ cup vegetable oil

¼ cup GF vinegar

2 tablespoons brown sugar

1 tablespoon honey

1 teaspoon GF hot sauce

1 teaspoon mustard

1 clove garlic, minced

1 tablespoon finely grated onion

Whisk all ingredients together.  In a medium saucepan over medium heat, bring to a boil.  Reduce heat to low, stirring frequently for about 10 minutes.  Serve cold as a dipping sauce or baste food during the last 10 minutes of grilling.

# Pumpkin Seed Sauce

1 cup raw pumpkin seeds (pepitas)

3 medium tomatoes

2 whole cloves garlic

½ cup GF chicken broth

½ cup fresh cilantro or parsley, loosely packed

2 serrano peppers, chopped

½ teaspoon salt

½ teaspoon pepper

Preheat oven to 400°. On a baking sheet roast the tomatoes for 25-30 minutes. Add the whole garlic cloves during the last 5 minutes of cooking. Meanwhile, in a dry skillet over medium heat roast the pumpkin seeds, stirring constantly for 2-3 minutes. The seeds will swell and begin to pop. In a food processor or blender combine the seeds, tomatoes, garlic, peppers and cilantro or parsley. Blend well until the mixture forms a paste. Slowly add the GF chicken broth until the sauce reaches the desired consistency. Warm sauce over medium heat until heated thoroughly. Serve over chicken, seafood or vegetables.

*This recipe is from Barbara Ambrose and Emilio Tobón*

# Fruit and Dessert Sauces

*The following sauces can be used as toppings for cakes, ice cream, waffles or pancakes*

## Apple Raisin Sauce

3 medium apples, peeled and coarsely chopped

2 cups apple juice

1 teaspoon cinnamon

1 tablespoon cornstarch

2 tablespoons cold water

¼ cup raisins

In a medium saucepan, combine all ingredients except the corn starch and water. Bring to a boil and reduce heat to low. Simmer 10-15 minutes until apples are soft. Whisk together corn starch and water in a small bowl. Slowly add to apples and cook, stirring another 2-3 minutes. Serve hot or cold.

## Blueberry Sauce

2 cups fresh or frozen blueberries, thawed

½ cup water

¼ cup sugar

1 tablespoon lemon juice

1 tablespoon corn starch

2 tablespoons cold water

In a medium saucepan, combine all ingredients except the corn starch and 2 tablespoons of water. Bring to a boil and reduce heat to low, simmering 3-5 minutes until liquid is reduced. Whisk together corn starch and water in a small bowl. Slowly add to blueberries and cook, stirring another 2-3 minutes. Serve hot or cold.

# Fruit and Dessert Sauces

## Ginger Pear Sauce

1 tablespoon butter

2 ripe pears- peeled, cored and chopped

½ cup water

2 tablespoons brown sugar

1 tablespoon lemon juice

1 teaspoon lemon zest

1 teaspoon ginger

Melt butter in a medium saucepan over medium heat. Add pears, stirring for 3-4 minutes. Stir in the water, brown sugar, lemon juice, lemon zest and ginger. Cover and cook over low heat until pears are soft, about 10-15 minutes. Mash with a fork or in a blender or food processor. Serve warm or cold.

## Strawberry Sauce

1 pint fresh strawberries

2 tablespoons orange juice

1 tablespoon sugar

Slice strawberries and heat in a medium sauce pan with orange juice and sugar. Stir constantly over medium heat for 5-6 minutes, until the mixture has thickened slightly. Best served warm.

# Fruit and Dessert Sauces

## Rhubarb Sauce

2 cups fresh rhubarb, chopped

½ cup sugar

½ cup orange juice

In a medium saucepan, bring all ingredients to a boil.  Reduce heat and simmer on low for 15-20 minutes until rhubarb has softened and sauce is thickened.  Serve warm or cold.

## Caramel Sauce

1 cup brown sugar

½ cup heavy cream or half-n-half

¼ cup light corn syrup

1 tablespoon butter

Heat all ingredients in a medium saucepan over medium heat, stirring constantly. When mixture starts to boil, reduce heat to low and simmer, stirring another 5 minutes.  Serve warm.

# Fruit and Dessert Sauces

## Chocolate Peanut Sauce

¾ cup milk

1/3 cup sugar

2 ounces semi-sweet chocolate

½ cup GF peanut butter (chunky or smooth)

In a medium saucepan over medium heat, melt the milk, sugar and chocolate, stirring constantly. When the chocolate is melted, remove from heat and whisk in peanut butter. Serve warm.

## Tropical Banana Sauce

1/3 cup flaked coconut

1 tablespoon butter

¼ cup brown sugar

¼ cup rum

¼ teaspoon cinnamon

3 bananas, peeled and sliced

In a medium skillet, toast the coconut over medium heat until light brown. Remove and cool. In a small saucepan, heat the butter, sugar, rum and cinnamon until it just comes to a boil. Add the bananas and cook until the bananas are heated through. Sprinkle with the toasted coconut.

*"It is not good for all our wishes to be filled; through sickness we recognize the value of health; through evil, the value of good; through hunger, the value of food; through exertion, the value of rest."*

*~Dorothy Canfield Fisher*

# Breads and Muffins

# Blueberry Corn Muffins

1 cup cornmeal

1 cup buttermilk*

¾ cup GF flour

¼ teaspoon xanthan gum

½ teaspoon baking soda

½ teaspoon GF baking powder

¼ teaspoon salt

1 egg, slightly beaten

1 tablespoon butter, melted

½ cup blueberries

¼ teaspoon cinnamon

For a smoother consistency, soak cornmeal in buttermilk for at least one hour before beginning. Preheat oven to 450°. In a medium bowl, stir together GF flour, xanthan gum, baking soda, baking powder, salt and cinnamon. In a separate large bowl, mix together cornmeal/buttermilk, egg and butter until well blended. Stir in dry ingredients until just combined. Lightly coat muffin tins with GF cooking spray or use muffin papers and fill 2/3 full. Bake for 10-12 minutes.

*Can substitute butter milk with 1 cup milk whisked with 1 tablespoon lemon juice.

# Zucchini Bread

*Bread:*

½ cup chopped walnuts

2 cups grated zucchini

½ cup vegetable oil

½ cup applesauce

2 cups sugar

3 eggs

2 teaspoons GF vanilla

1 teaspoon baking soda

¼ teaspoon GF baking powder

3 cups GF flour

3 teaspoons xanthan gum

3 teaspoons cinnamon

1 teaspoon salt

½ teaspoon nutmeg (optional)

*Topping (optional):*

½ cup brown sugar

½ cup GF flour

1 teaspoon cinnamon

2 tablespoons cold butter

Preheat oven to 350°. Grease and GF flour or use GF cooking spray to coat two 8in loaf pans. In a medium bowl, combine the GF flour, xanthan gum, cinnamon, salt, walnuts, baking powder, baking soda, and nutmeg; set aside. In a medium bowl, beat the eggs until light and frothy. Mix in the oil, applesauce, sugar, zucchini and vanilla. Stir in the dry ingredients and divide between the two loaf pans.

For the topping, combine the brown sugar, flour, cinnamon and cold butter with a pastry blender or fork until crumbly. Spread topping over the two loaf pans and bake for 60-75 minutes. Let cool before slicing.

# Apple Muffins

1 2/3 cup GF flour

1 ¼ teaspoon xanthan gum

½ cup brown sugar

¼ cup granulated sugar

2 ½ teaspoons GF baking powder

¼ teaspoon baking soda

¼ teaspoon salt

1 teaspoon cinnamon

½ teaspoon nutmeg

1 egg, beaten

1 cup milk

¼ cup applesauce

1 cup finely chopped apple

Preheat oven to 400°. In a large bowl, combine the GF flour, xanthan gum, brown sugar, granulated sugar, cinnamon, nutmeg, baking powder and salt. Make a well in the center of the mixture. In a separate bowl, whisk the egg, milk and applesauce together. Pour into the flour mixture and stir until just moistened. Gently fold in the chopped apple. Lightly coat the muffin tins with GF cooking spray or use muffin papers and fill the cups 2/3 full. Bake for 20-25 minutes or until a toothpick inserted into the center comes out clean.

# Cinnamon Raisin Beer Bread

3 cups GF flour

3 teaspoons xanthan gum

1 cup granulated sugar

¼ cup brown sugar

2 teaspoons cinnamon

3 teaspoons GF baking powder

1 ½ teaspoons salt

1 teaspoon GF vanilla

1 cup raisins

1 (12oz.) bottle of GF beer

Preheat oven to 350°. In a medium mixing bowl, combine the GF flour, xanthan gum, granulated sugar, brown sugar, cinnamon, baking powder and salt. Make a well in the center and slowly pour in the GF beer and vanilla. Stir until just combined. Fold in the raisins. Pour into an ungreased 8 inch loaf pan. Bake for 1 hour, or until a toothpick inserted into the center comes out clean. Cool before serving.

# Banana Bread

2 cups GF flour

2 teaspoons xanthan gum

1 teaspoon baking soda

¼ teaspoon salt

½ cup butter

¾ cup brown sugar

¼ cup granulated sugar

1 teaspoon cinnamon

2 eggs, beaten

2 1/3 cup mashed over-ripe bananas (about 5 or 6 medium)

1 teaspoon GF vanilla

½ cup chopped walnut (optional)

*Topping (optional):*

¼ cup brown sugar

½ teaspoon cinnamon

1 tablespoon butter

Preheat oven to 350° and grease or lightly spray an 8 inch loaf pan. In a large bowl, combine the GF flour, xanthan gum, baking soda, salt, and cinnamon. In a separate bowl, cream the butter with the granulated and brown sugar. Stir in the eggs, banana and vanilla until well blended. Stir banana mixture into flour mixture until just moistened. Don't overmix. Fold in chopped walnuts and pour into loaf pan. Mix together topping with a pastry blender or fork until crumbly and sprinkle over top of bread. Bake for 60-75 minutes. You may need to cover with foil for the last 10-15 minutes of baking to prevent the bread from drying out. Cool completely.

# *Scones*

2 cups GF flour

¾ teaspoon xanthan gum

2 tablespoons sugar

1 tablespoon GF baking powder

½ teaspoon salt

3 tablespoons butter, cold and cut into pieces

1 egg, beaten

½ cup milk

Preheat oven to 450°. In a large mixing bowl, combine the GF flour, xanthan gum, sugar, baking powder and salt. With a pastry blender or fork, cut in the cold butter until it resembles coarse crumbs, being careful not to overmix the butter. Stir in the egg and gradually add the milk until a thick dough is formed (you may need up to ¾ cup). Roll out the dough on a GF floured workspace. Roll out to ¾ inch thick and cut into 2 inch circles with a cookie cutter. Place the scones on a baking sheet, 1 inch apart. Brush the tops with milk and bake for 10-15 minutes until golden brown.

*Lemon Scones:* Increase the amount of sugar by 1 tablespoon. After adding the egg to the recipe, stir in the juice and zest of 1 lemon.

*Chocolate Chip Scones:* After adding the egg to the recipe, stir in ½ cup GF white or GF semi-sweet chocolate chips.

*Cheddar Scones:* After adding the egg, stir in 1 cup grated cheddar cheese to the recipe.

*Fruit Scones:* With the dry ingredients, stir in ½ teaspoon cinnamon. After adding the egg, stir in ½ cup dried cranberries, raisins or cranberries to the recipe.

# Lemon Poppy Seed Loaf

1 cup GF flour

1 teaspoon xanthan gum

½ teaspoon GF baking powder

½ cup sugar

8 tablespoons butter

2 eggs

Zest of 1 lemon

3 tablespoons poppy seeds

*Topping:*

¼ cup sugar

¼ cup lemon juice

Preheat oven to 350°. Grease or lightly spray a 9 inch loaf pan. In a small bowl, combine the flour, xanthan gum and baking powder. In a mixer, cream the butter with sugar. Add the eggs, one at a time. Stir in the flour mix, lemon zest and poppy seeds. Pour into the loaf pan and bake for 35-40 minutes. In a small saucepan, over low heat, dissolve the lemon juice and sugar. While the loaf is cooling in the pan, poke holes in the top and pour the lemon mixture over the top. Cool completely.

# Gingerbread

1 ½ cups GF flour

1 teaspoon xanthan gum

½ teaspoon GF baking powder

½ teaspoon baking soda

1 teaspoon salt

1 ½ teaspoon ginger

¼ teaspoon cloves

¾ teaspoon cinnamon

1/3 cup vegetable oil

½ cup brown sugar

1 egg, beaten

½ cup molasses

½ cup boiling water

Preheat oven to 350°. Grease or lightly spray an 8x8 inch baking dish with GF cooking spray. In a large bowl, stir together the flour, xanthan gum, baking powder, baking soda, salt, ginger, cloves, cinnamon and brown sugar. Make a well in the mix and pour in the oil and beaten egg. Mix together the boiling water and molasses and add to the mix. Stir until smooth and pour into pan. Bake for 35-40 minutes. Serve plain or top with brown sugar frosting (page 157), whipped cream (page 158) or a fruit sauce (page 106-108).

# Cornbread

2 cups cornmeal

1 ½ cups buttermilk*

1 ½ teaspoons GF baking powder

½ teaspoon baking soda

1 teaspoon salt

1 egg, lightly beaten

2 tablespoons vegetable oil

¼ cup sugar**

Preheat oven to 400°. Generously grease an 8x8 inch baking dish***. In a medium bowl, mix together the cornmeal, baking powder, baking soda, sugar and salt. Stir in the egg, vegetable oil and buttermilk. Pour into the baking dish and bake for 20-25 minutes. Cool completely before cutting.

Before pouring into the baking sheet, fold in any of your favorite ingredients, including: ½ teaspoon crushed red pepper flakes, ½ cup finely chopped onion, ½ cup chopped green pepper or ½ cup grated cheddar cheese.

*Can substitute with 1 ½ cups of milk whisked with 1 ½ tablespoons lemon juice

**If making cornbread for stuffing, omit the sugar

***Can make muffins, by decreasing baking time to 15 minutes

# Cookies

# Chocolate Chip Cookies

1 ¾ cup GF flour

1 teaspoon xanthan gum

½ cup finely chopped or pureed walnuts

1 (3.4 oz.) package vanilla instant pudding

1 teaspoon baking soda

1 teaspoon salt

¾ cup brown sugar

¾ cup granulated sugar

¾ cup butter (12 tablespoons)

2 eggs

1 teaspoon GF vanilla

1 (12oz.) package GF semi-sweet chocolate chips

Preheat oven to 350°. In a food processor or chopper, finely grind nuts with ¼ cup granulated sugar. In a medium bowl, mix together the GF flour, xanthan gum, baking soda, ground nuts and set aside. In a mixer or by hand, cream the remaining granulated sugar, brown sugar and butter together. Add the eggs and vanilla, mixing until just blended. Slowly add the flour mixture and stir until just blended. Stir in the chocolate chips and drop by rounded teaspoonfuls on an ungreased cookie sheet 2inches apart. Bake for 12-14 minutes. Cool on a wire rack.

# Almond Cookies

1 ½ cups finely ground almonds

½ cup sugar

1 egg, beaten

1 teaspoon GF almond or GF vanilla extract

¼ cup sugar for dusting

Preheat oven to 350°. Grind almonds and sugar in a food processor or chopper. (The sugar will keep the almonds from forming a paste and clumping.) Stir in the egg and almond or vanilla extract until blended. Roll ½ inch balls in sugar and place 2 inches apart on an ungreased cookie sheet. Bake for 12-15 minutes. Cool on a wire rack. Also good dipped in melted chocolate.

# Coconut Nests

1 ¼ cup GF semi-sweet chocolate chips

1 cup flaked coconut

1 cup GF chocolate candy eggs or GF jelly beans

Melt chocolate in a double boiler or carefully in a microwave. Stir in coconut and shape into golf ball sized balls. Press your thumb in the middle of each ball to hollow out a nest. Top with chocolate candies or jelly beans. Allow to cool completely.

# Sugar Cookies

1 cup granulated sugar

½ cup butter (8 tablespoons)

1 egg, beaten

½ cup buttermilk*

2 cups GF flour

½ teaspoon xanthan gum

½ teaspoon salt

½ teaspoon baking soda

½ teaspoon GF baking powder

1 teaspoon GF vanilla

¼ cup coarse sugar

Preheat oven to 375°. In a medium bowl, blend together the GF flour, xanthan gum, baking soda, baking powder and salt and set aside. In mixer or by hand, blend together the butter and sugar. Mix in the egg, vanilla and buttermilk. Gradually blend in the dry ingredients, being careful not to overmix. Roll into teaspoon sized balls. Bake 8-10 minutes or until light brown. Sprinkle with coarse sugar or top with your favorite frosting.

*Can substitute with ½ cup milk whisked with ½ tablespoon lemon juice.

*This was adapted from a recipe by Edna Mahaney.*

# Peanut Butter Cookies

2 cups peanut butter

1 ½ cups sugar

2 eggs

1 teaspoon GF vanilla extract

½ cup sugar for dusting (optional)

About 30 Hershey's Kisses, unwrapped (optional)

Preheat oven to 350°. Mix all ingredients except reserved ¼ cup sugar in a large bowl until well combined. Form into 1 inch balls and roll in sugar. Bake for 12-15 minutes. Immediately press a Hershey's Kiss into the top when taken out of the oven. (If you prefer plain peanut butter cookies, flatten in a criss-cross pattern with a fork before baking. Cool completely.

# Blonde Brownies

1 ¼ cups Beth's All Purpose Flour

¾ teaspoon GF baking powder

½ cup (8 tablespoons) butter, softened

1 cup brown sugar

2 eggs

1 teaspoon GF vanilla

¾ cup toasted pecans

½ cup GF semi-sweet chocolate chips

Preheat oven to 350°. Coat a 9 inch square pan with GF cooking spray. In a small bowl, stir together GF flour and baking powder and set aside. With a mixer or by hand, beat butter and brown sugar until light and fluffy. Add eggs and vanilla and beat well. Add the flour and baking powder and stir until thoroughly combined. Fold in the pecans and chocolate chips. Spread evenly into prepared pan and bake 35-40 minutes. Allow to cool completely in the pan before cutting into squares.

*Recipe reprinted with permission from Beth Hillson, founder of Gluten-Free Pantry at www.glutenfree.com*

# Double Chocolate Chip Cookies

4 oz. GF unsweetened chocolate

2 cups GF semi-sweet chocolate chips

2 tablespoons unsweetened cocoa powder

1 cup sugar

1 ½ teaspoons GF vanilla

6 tablespoons butter

¼ teaspoon GF baking powder

¼ teaspoon salt

½ cup GF flour

¼ teaspoon xanthan gum

3 eggs

In a small bowl mix together the flour, xanthan gum, cocoa, baking powder and salt and set aside.  In a double boiler or carefully in the microwave, melt the unsweetened chocolate, butter and 1 cup semi-sweet chocolate chips.  Cool slightly. With a mixer or by hand, beat the sugar and eggs for 2 minutes.  Mix in the vanilla. Stir in the melted chocolate and then the flour mixture until well blended.  Fold in the remaining 1 cup of chocolate chips.  Cover and chill in the refrigerator for at least 1 hour.

Preheat oven to 350°.  Shape dough into 1 inch balls and place 2 inches apart on an ungreased baking sheet.  Bake for 10 minutes. Cool completely on a wire rack.

# Coconut Macaroons

2 egg whites

1/8 teaspoon salt

1/8 teaspoon cream of tartar

1 teaspoon GF vanilla

¾ cup sugar

1 ½ cups shredded coconut

Preheat oven to 300°. Lightly spray a cookie sheet with GF cooking spray. Beat egg whites, salt and cream of tartar until soft peaks form. Add vanilla and sugar until stiff peaks form. Fold in coconut. Drop by teaspoonfuls 2 inches apart on cookie sheet. Bake for 25 minutes and cool completely.

# Layer Bars

1 (7oz.) package of flaked coconut

1 cup GF white chocolate chips

1 cup GF semi-sweet chocolate chips

1 cup finely chopped nuts

1 cup GF cookies, finely ground*

1 (14oz.) can sweetened condensed milk

Preheat oven to 350°. Press 2/3 of the coconut mixed with the cookie crumbs into the bottom of an 8x8 inch or 9x11 inch baking dish. Top with the chocolate chips and nuts. Pour sweetened condensed milk over the top and sprinkle with the remaining coconut. Bake for 20 minutes. Cool completely before cutting into squares.

*GF arrowroot or animal crackers work well in this recipe.

# Halfmoon Cookies

3 ¾ cup GF flour

1 teaspoon xanthan gum

1 teaspoon GF baking powder

2 teaspoons baking soda

2 ¼ cups sugar

1 cup butter, cut into pieces

¾ cup unsweetened cocoa powder

¼ teaspoon salt

2 eggs

1 teaspoon GF vanilla extract

1 ½ cups milk

Preheat oven to 350°. Lightly spray a cookie sheet with GF cooking spray. In a medium bowl, combine the GF flour, xanthan gum, baking powder and baking soda and set aside. With a mixer, cream the butter, sugar, cocoa and salt until fluffy. Add eggs and vanilla and continue to beat. Add ½ cup milk and ½ of the flour mix, and beat until smooth. Repeat with remaining milk and flour mix. Spoon batter onto a cookie sheet making 3 inch round circles that are 2 inches apart. Bake until set, about 12 minutes and cool completely.

Spread the flat side of the cookie with 1 tablespoon of warm fudge icing. When the icing has cooled, spread the other half of the cookie with 1 tablespoon buttercream frosting. These cookies freeze well.

# Halfmoon Cookie Frostings

*Fudge Icing:*

3 ½ ounces GF bittersweet chocolate

3 ½ ounces GF semisweet chocolate

1 tablespoon butter

4 1/3 cup confectioners or powdered sugar

2 tablespoons corn syrup

1 teaspoon GF vanilla

1/8 teaspoon salt

6 tablespoons boiling water

*Buttercream Frosting:*

7 cups confectioners or powdered sugar

1 cup butter, room temperature, cut into pieces

½ cup vegetable shortening

7 tablespoons milk

1 teaspoon GF vanilla extract

1/8 teaspoon salt

*Fudge Icing:* Melt the chocolates and butter in a double boiler over medium-low heat. Remove from heat and stir in the confectioners sugar, corn syrup, GF vanilla, salt and boiling water until smooth. The icing should fall from the spoon in thick ribbons. If needed, thin with more boiling water. Keep warm in a double boiler over low heat.

*Buttercream Frosting:* With a mixer, beat the sugar, butter, shortening, milk, vanilla and salt in a bowl and beat on low until combined. Increase to medium speed and beat until light and fluffy.

*If you run out of one flavor of frosting, you can make "full moon" cookies (all buttercream) or "new moon" cookies (all fudge icing).

# Chocolate Peanut Butter Bars

½ cup butter

1 teaspoon GF vanilla extract

½ cup brown sugar

2 cups GF peanut butter

2 ½ cups confectioners or powdered sugar

2 cups GF semi-sweet chocolate chips

Melt butter and mix with confectioners sugar and brown sugar. Stir in vanilla and peanut butter. Press into the bottom of an 8x11 inch pan. Melt the chocolate chips in a double boiler over low-medium heat or carefully in the microwave. Spread the chocolate on top of the peanut butter mixture and cool completely. Cut into 1-2 inch squares (they are very sweet).

# Cranberry Nut Bars

*Crust:*

1 cup GF Beth's All Purpose Baking Flour

½ cup chopped nuts

½ cup brown sugar

½ teaspoon salt

6 tablespoons cold butter

*Filling:*

2 teaspoons GF Beth's All Purpose Baking Flour

½ teaspoon baking powder

2 beaten eggs

1 cup sugar

1 tablespoon milk

1 tablespoon GF vanilla

1 cup fresh cranberries, chopped

½ cup unsweetened coconut

½ cup chopped nuts

1 ½ teaspoons grated orange peel

Preheat oven to 350°. In a mixing bowl, combine the flour, nuts, brown sugar and salt. Cut in butter with a pastry blender or fork until mixture is crumbly. Press into an 8x8 inch baking dish that has been sprayed with GF cooking spray. Bake for 20 minutes. Meanwhile, in a large bowl combine the GF flour and baking powder. Add eggs, sugar, milk and vanilla. Fold in cranberries, coconut, nuts and orange peel. Pour filling mixture over crust. Return to oven and bake an additional 25 minutes. Cool completely on a wire rack and cut into bars.

*Recipe reprinted with permission from Beth Hillson, founder of Gluten-Free Pantry at www.glutenfree.com*

# Spice Cookies

2 cups GF flour

½ teaspoon xanthan gum

1 cup sugar

¾ cup butter

¼ cup molasses

1 egg

2 teaspoons baking soda

2 teaspoons ginger

1 teaspoon cinnamon

¼ teaspoon salt

¼ teaspoon cloves

¼ cup sugar for dusting

Preheat oven to 350°. In a medium bowl, combine the GF flour, xanthan gum, baking soda, cloves, ginger, cinnamon and salt and set aside. With a mixer or by hand, beat the butter and sugar until fluffy. Add the egg and molasses, beating until well combined. Mix in the dry ingredients. Roll into 1 inch balls and roll in sugar. Flatten the cookies slightly and bake for 8-10 minutes. Cool completely on a wire rack. Top with your favorite cookie icing (recipes on pages 155-157).

# Chocolate Thin Mints

*Cookies:*

1 ¼ cups GF flour

¼ teaspoon xanthan gum

½ cup unsweetened cocoa powder

¼ teaspoon salt

½ cup (8 tablespoons) butter, softened

1 cup sugar

1 egg

1 teaspoon mint extract

*Topping:*

½ cup GF semi-sweet chocolate chips

¼ cup butter

In a small bowl, combine the GF flour, cocoa and salt and set aside. With a mixer or by hand, beat the butter and sugar until creamy. Add the egg and mint extract and mix until well combined. Slowly beat in the flour mixture until well combined. Divide the dough in half. On wax paper, roll each half into a 1 ½ inch diameter tube. Wrap each tube in waxed paper and refrigerate at least 5-6 hours.

Preheat oven to 350°. Slice cookies with a very sharp knife to about ¼ inch thick slices. Place on ungreased cookie sheets, about 2 inches apart. Bake 10-12 minutes. Cool completely and place in the refrigerator while making the topping.

For the topping, melt the butter and chocolate in a double boiler over low heat or carefully in the microwave. Dip cookies in the chocolate, shaking off an excess. Let cool and harden completely.

# Fig Newtons

2 ½ cups GF flour

½ teaspoon xanthan gum

½ teaspoon salt

½ teaspoon cinnamon

½ teaspoon baking soda

2/3 cup butter

1 cup brown sugar

2 eggs

1 teaspoon GF vanilla

*Filling:*

3 cups finely chopped fresh figs*

¼ cup water

¼ cup sugar

2 tablespoons lemon juice

For the dough: Mix together the GF flour, xanthan gum, salt, cinnamon, and baking soda and set aside. With a mixer, cream the butter and brown sugar until fluffy. Beat in the eggs and vanilla until well combined. Slowly mix in the flour mixture. Wrap the dough in plastic wrap and chill for 2-3 hours.

For the filling: Stir the figs, water, brown sugar and lemon juice in a medium saucepan. Simmer on low-medium heat for 5-7 minutes or until the mixture thickens. Cool slightly.

Preheat the oven to 350°. Roll out small pieces of the dough at a time, making a ¼ inch thick piece that is about 2 x 3 inches long. Place a heaping teaspoon full of fig mixture in the center of the dough and fold the dough around the filling. Flatten the cookies slightly to create a seam. Place fig newtons on a cookie sheet about 1 inch apart. Bake for about 12 minutes or until lightly browned. Cool completely.

*If you cannot find fresh figs, use 2 cups of dried golden figs and increase the water to 1 cup. If you are chopping figs in a food processor, add a small amount of the sugar to prevent them from sticking together.

# Chocolate Peanut Butter Cookies

1 (12oz.) package GF semi-sweet chocolate chips

2 ounces unsweetened GF chocolate

2 tablespoons butter

¼ cup GF flour

¼ teaspoon GF baking powder

1/8 teaspoon salt

2 eggs

2/3 cup sugar

1 teaspoon GF vanilla

½ cup GF peanut butter

Preheat oven to 350°. In a double boiler over low-medium heat or carefully in the microwave, melt 1 cup semisweet chocolate chips, 2 ounces unsweetened chocolate and butter together. Cool slightly. In a small bowl, combine the GF flour, baking powder, and salt and set aside. Add the eggs, sugar, vanilla and peanut butter to the chocolate and beat well. Stir in the flour mix until well combined. Fold in the remaining chocolate chips and drop by teaspoonfuls onto an ungreased cookie sheet, 2 inches apart. Bake for 8-10 minutes and cool on a wire rack.

# Pumpkin Cookies

1 cup canned pumpkin

¾ cup granulated sugar

¼ cup brown sugar

½ cup butter

1 egg

2 cups GF flour

¾ teaspoon xanthan gum

2 teaspoons GF baking powder

1 teaspoon baking soda

1 teaspoon cinnamon

½ teaspoon nutmeg

½ teaspoon cloves

½ teaspoon salt

1 teaspoon GF vanilla

1 cup GF semi-sweet chocolate chips (optional)

*Icing (optional):*

2 cups confectioners or powdered sugar

3 tablespoons milk

1 teaspoon GF vanilla

Preheat oven to 350°. In a medium bowl, combine the GF flour, xanthan gum, cinnamon, nutmeg, cloves, baking powder, baking soda and salt and set aside. With a mixer or by hand, cream together the butter, granulated sugar and brown sugar. Add the egg, vanilla and pumpkin and beat until creamy. Gradually mix in the flour mixture until well combined. Fold in the chocolate chips. Drop by tablespoonfuls onto an ungreased cookie sheet. Bake for 15-20 minutes. Cool completely and drizzle with the icing below, or use cream cheese icing (page 155).

To make the icing: Mix together the confectioners sugar, vanilla and milk. Add an additional tablespoon of milk at a time to get the desired consistency.

*"One of the very nicest things about life is the way we must regularly stop whatever it is we are doing and devote our attention to eating."*

~Luciano Pavarotti

# Cakes and Pies

# Strawberry Torte

1 cup GF flour

½ teaspoon xanthan gum

1 ¼ teaspoon GF baking powder

¼ teaspoon salt

½ cup milk

1 ½ cup sugar

1 teaspoon GF vanilla

½ cup butter

4 eggs, separated at room temperature

*Filling:*

2 cups fresh strawberries cut into slices*

1 cup whipped cream

Preheat oven to 375°. Grease and GF flour two 8 inch cake pans. In a small bowl, combine the GF flour, xanthan gum, baking powder and salt and set aside. Cream ½ cup sugar with the butter until fluffy. Mix in the beaten egg yolks. Mix in the flour and milk slowly, alternating with small amounts of each. Stir in the vanilla and divide between the cake pans.

With a clean and dry mixer, beat the egg whites until stiff. Gradually beat in 1 cup of sugar. Spread half of the mixture over each cake. Bake for 25 minutes or until the meringue is lightly browned. Cool completely in pans on wire racks.

Mix together strawberries and whipped cream (directions on page 158). Place one cake, with meringue side down and top with strawberry mix. Place the second cake on top with the meringue side up. Refrigerate until serving.

*Can substitute with blueberries, mixed berries or drained pineapple.

*Pictured on back cover.*

# Chocolate Hazelnut Torte

6 ounces GF semi-sweet chocolate

¾ cup butter

4 eggs, separated at room temperature

1/8 teaspoon salt

¾ cup sugar

¾ cup finely ground hazelnuts

2 tablespoons brewed coffee

¼ cup whole hazelnuts for topping

Preheat oven to 375°. Grease and GF flour the bottom of an 8 inch springform pan. In a double boiler over low-medium heat or carefully in the microwave, melt the chocolate and butter. Cool slightly. Beat the egg whites and salt on high speed until stiff and set aside. Beat the egg yolks and sugar on medium speed until lemon colored. Stir the egg yolks into the chocolate mixture with the hazelnuts and coffee. Gently fold in the egg whites and pour into pan. Bake for 40-45 minutes, or until the top of the torte is dry (a toothpick poked in the top will still come out slightly moist). Cool completely before removing from pan. Top with hazelnuts and then cover with chocolate ganache (recipe on page 156).

# Chocolate Torte

8 tablespoons butter

½ tablespoon GF flour

9 ounces bittersweet chocolate

6 eggs, separated at room temperature

1 cup sugar, divided

6 tablespoons corn starch

Preheat oven to 350°.  Grease and GF flour the bottom of an 8 inch springform pan. In a double boiler over low-medium heat or carefully in the microwave, melt the chocolate with the butter and cool slightly.  Beat the egg whites with ½ cup sugar until soft peaks form and set aside.  In a separate bowl, beat the egg yolks with ½ cup sugar on medium high speed until thick and lemon-colored.  The yolks should triple in volume, about 5 minutes.  Beat in the corn starch and vanilla extract.  Stir in the melted chocolate with the egg yolks until well combined.  Gently fold in the egg whites until just combined.  Pour into the pan and bake for 30-35 minutes.  Cool completely before removing from the springform pan.  Top with whipped cream (recipes page 158) or chocolate ganache (recipe on page 156).

# Lemon Ricotta Cheesecake

1 GF gingersnap crust recipe (page 160)

2 (15 oz.) containers ricotta cheese

½ cup sugar

½ cup milk

2 teaspoons GF vanilla

4 eggs

*Topping:*

2/3 cup water

1/3 cup lemon juice

1/3 cup sugar

1 tablespoon corn starch

1 tablespoon grated lemon zest

Preheat oven to 325°. Press GF gingersnap crust into the bottom of a 9 inch springform pan. Put the ricotta cheese in a blender or food processor and blend until smooth. Stir in the sugar, milk, vanilla and eggs and mix until well combined. Pour into the springform pan and bake for 60-65 minutes, or until set. Cool completely in the pan.

In a small saucepan, heat the water, lemon juice, sugar, corn starch and lemon zest over low-medium heat. Stir constantly until the topping thickens and pour over cheesecake. Allow to cool completely before removing from the springform pan. Refrigerate for at least 4 hours before serving.

# *Pumpkin Cheesecake*

1 GF gingersnap, almond or pecan crust recipe (pages 159-160)

3 (8oz.) packages cream cheese

½ cup granulated sugar

½ cup brown sugar

½ cup sour cream

3 eggs

1 teaspoon GF vanilla extract

2 teaspoons cinnamon

½ teaspoon nutmeg

1/8 teaspoon cloves

½ teaspoon ginger

1 (16oz.) can pumpkin

Preheat oven to 325°. Press the prepared crust recipe into the bottom of a 9 inch springform pan. With a mixer, beat the cream cheese, sour cream, brown sugar and granulated sugar together until smooth. Add the spices and pumpkin and continue beating. On low speed, beat in the eggs until well combined. Pour over the crust and bake for 60-75 minutes. Cool completely before removing from the springform pan. Refrigerate for 3-4 hours before serving.

# Chocolate Cheesecake

1 GF chocolate cookie crust recipe (page 160)

3 (8oz.) packages cream cheese

¾ cup sugar

3 eggs

½ cup sour cream

1 teaspoon GF vanilla

1 tablespoon brewed coffee

1/8 cup GF flour

1/8 cup cocoa powder

1 cup GF semi-sweet chocolate chips

Preheat oven to 350°. Press the prepared cookie crust into the bottom of an 8 inch springform pan. With a mixer, beat the cream cheese and sugar together until smooth. Add the GF flour and cocoa powder and beat until well combined. Mix in the eggs one at a time with the GF vanilla and coffee until all ingredients are well blended. Stir in the chocolate chips and pour into the prepared pan. Bake for 55-60 minutes or until the cheesecake is set. Cool completely before removing from the springform pan. Refrigerate at least 3-4 hours before serving.

# Boston Cream Pie

*Cake:*

4 eggs

1 cup sugar

1 cup GF flour

¾ teaspoon xanthan

¾ teaspoon GF baking powder

¼ teaspoon salt

¼ cup water

½ teaspoon GF vanilla extract

1 teaspoon lemon juice

*Filling:*

1 ½ cups milk

1 (3.4oz.) package instant vanilla pudding mix

*Icing:*

Chocolate ganache recipe (page 156)

Preheat oven to 350°. Grease and GF flour two 8 inch round cake pans. In a medium bowl, combine the GF flour, xanthan gum, baking powder and salt and set aside. Beat the eggs on medium speed until they are thick and lemon-colored. Gradually beat in the sugar slowly. Continue beating until the eggs are very thick, about 5 minutes. Whisk together the water, lemon juice and vanilla in a small bowl. Add the GF flour mix and the lemon juice mix to the eggs, and beat an additional 1-2 minutes. Divide the batter into the two cake pans and bake for 25 minutes or until the cake is set. Cool completely. Prepare the vanilla pudding with 1 ½ cups of milk. Place one cake on a plate, spoon on the pudding and top with the other cake. Pour over the ganache and allow the chocolate to harden. Refrigerate until serving.

# Carrot Cake

2 cups sugar

2 cups GF flour

2 teaspoons xanthan gum

2 teaspoons baking soda

1 teaspoon salt

3 teaspoons cinnamon

1 cup vegetable oil

½ cup applesauce

4 eggs

3 cups grated carrots

½ cup crushed pineapple (optional)

1 teaspoon GF vanilla

1 cup finely chopped nuts (optional)

1 cup raisins (optional)

Preheat oven to 350°. Grease and GF flour two 8 inch round cake pans or one 9x13 inch cake pan. In a large bowl, mix together the GF flour, xanthan gum, sugar, baking soda, salt and cinnamon. Stir in the oil and applesauce. Add the eggs, one at a time and mix until just combined. Stir in the carrots, raisins, nuts, pineapple and vanilla. Mix until all are well combined. Pour into cake pans and bake for 45 minutes (two 8 inch round pans), or 60-65 minutes (one 9x13 inch pan). Watch the cake closely, as the added ingredients will adjust the baking times, check to make sure a toothpick inserted into the center of the cake comes out clean.

Layer the two 8 inch cakes with cream cheese frosting in the center and covering the entire cake. Frost the 9x13 inch cake with all of the cream cheese frosting (recipe page 155).

*Pictured on the front cover.*

# Angel Food Cake

12 egg whites, room temperature

1 ¼ teaspoons cream of tartar

¼ teaspoon salt

1 cup sugar

1 teaspoon GF vanilla

¾ cup GF flour

¼ teaspoon xanthan gum

2 tablespoons corn starch

Preheat oven to 375°. In a small bowl, mix together the GF flour, corn starch and xanthan gum and set aside. Beat the egg whites and add the cream of tartar and salt when the eggs are frothy. Continue beating until the egg whites form soft peaks. Gradually beat in the sugar and vanilla. Fold the flour mixture gently into the batter until well incorporated. Pour the cake batter into an ungreased 10-inch tube pan. Bake for 35-40 minutes. Remove from oven and turn pan upside down (balancing on a beer or wine bottle works well). Inverting the cake will help to keep it from collapsing. When the cake is completely cooled, gently run a thin knife around the outside of the pan and around the center tube to help remove the cake from the pan. Top with a fruit or dessert topping (recipes pages 106-109) or flavored whipped cream (page 158).

*Chocolate Angel Food Cake:* Reduce GF flour to ½ cup, keep the ¼ teaspoon xanthan gum and add ¼ cup of cocoa powder.

# Lemon Yogurt Pie

1 prepared GF gingersnap crust recipe (page 160)

2 eggs, separated at room temperature

2 cups plain yogurt

Zest of 1 lemon

1 tablespoon lemon juice

½ cup sugar

1 tablespoon GF flour

½ teaspoon salt

Preheat oven to 350°. Press the GF gingersnap crust into the bottom and up the sides of a 9 inch pie plate. Bake the crust for 15 minutes and cool completely.

Beat the egg whites with the salt until they form stiff peaks and set aside. In a separate bowl, beat the egg yolks. Mix in the yogurt, lemon zest, lemon juice, sugar and GF flour with the egg yolks. Gently fold in the egg whites, being careful not to overmix. Pour into the cooled pie crust and bake for 30-45 minutes. Cool completely and refrigerate for 3-4 hours before serving.

# Pumpkin Pie

1 recipe GF pie crust (pages 159-160)

3 eggs*

2 cups canned pumpkin

1 cup heavy or light cream*

½ cup brown sugar

1 teaspoon cinnamon

½ teaspoon ginger

¼ teaspoon cloves

½ teaspoon salt

Preheat oven to 350°. Press the crust into the bottom and sides of a 9 inch pie plate. Combine the eggs, cream and pumpkin. Mix until well blended. In a separate bowl, stir together the brown sugar, cinnamon, ginger, cloves and salt. Blend the mixture into the eggs, cream and pumpkin. Pour into the unbaked pie shell and bake for 50-55 minutes, or until the pumpkin is set.

*Make this recipe dairy free by using a prepackaged, GF-Dairy Free pie crust. Substitute the eggs and cream with 1 ½ (14 oz.) packages of extra firm tofu.

# *Pecan Pie*

1 prepared GF crust recipe (pages 159-160)

3 eggs

¼ cup sugar

1 teaspoon GF vanilla

1 cup light corn syrup

1 tablespoon butter, melted

1 cup pecans

Preheat oven to 375°. Press the GF crust into the bottom and sides of a 9 inch pie plate. Layer the pecans on the bottom of the unbaked pie shell. In a medium bowl, beat the eggs and sugar on medium speed for 2-3 minutes. Continue beating, and add the corn syrup, butter, and vanilla. Pour over pecans and bake for 40-50 minutes, or until the filling is set. Let cool completely before serving.

# Caramel Apple Pie

1 prepared GF pie crust recipe (pages 159-160)

6 cups apples, peeled, cored and thinly sliced

1 tablespoon lemon juice

½ cup sugar

½ teaspoon nutmeg

1 teaspoon cinnamon

¼ teaspoon salt

*Topping:*

12 GF caramel candies

¼ cup butter

2 tablespoons milk

Preheat oven to 375°.  Press the prepared pie crust into the bottom and sides of a 9 in pie plate.  In a large bowl, mix the apples with the lemon juice, sugar, nutmeg, cinnamon and salt.  Pour into the unbaked pie crust.  In a small saucepan over low heat, melt the milk, butter and caramels, stirring constantly.  When the mixture is smooth, immediately pour over the apples.  Bake for 30-35 minutes or until the apples are tender.

# Frostings and Icings

### Cream Cheese Frosting:

½ cup butter, melted

1 (8oz.) package cream cheese, softened

1 teaspoon GF vanilla

3 cups confectioners or powdered sugar

With a mixer, combine the butter, cream cheese and vanilla and beat until smooth. Gradually add the sugar, beating on low until smooth.

### Cream Cheese Icing:

½ cup cream cheese, softened

2 tablespoons butter, melted

1 ½ cups confectioners or powdered sugar

Combine all ingredients in a medium bowl until well blended.

### Lemon Glaze:

4 tablespoons lemon juice

2 ½ cups confectioners or powdered sugar

Combine lemon juice and sugar until smooth.

# Frostings and Icings

## Chocolate Frosting:

2 ½ cups confectioners or powdered sugar

1 egg

2 tablespoons water

¼ cup sugar

¼ teaspoon salt

½ cup butter

1 teaspoon GF vanilla

4 ounces unsweetened chocolate

With a mixer, beat the confectioners sugar and egg until smooth. In a medium saucepan, combine the water, sugar and salt and bring to a boil over medium heat. Boil for 1 minute and cool slightly. Slowly pour the water and sugar into the egg mix, beating constantly. Melt the butter with the chocolate and stir until smooth. Add the chocolate and vanilla to the frosting and beat until creamy.

## Chocolate Ganache/Icing:

8 ounces GF semi-sweet chocolate

¾ cup heavy cream

2 tablespoons butter

Pour the chocolate chips into a heat-proof bowl and set aside. In a saucepan, heat the butter and milk, stirring, until just before the milk comes to a boil. Pour over the chocolate, cover and let stand for 5 minutes. Stir until smooth.

To make truffles: Refrigerate chocolate for 1 hour. Roll into teaspoon size balls (a melon baler works well) and dip in cocoa powder, confectioner's sugar, finely chopped nuts or finely chopped coconut. Cool completely. You may need to re-chill the chocolate if it begins to melt while making the truffles. Store in an air-tight container for up to one month.

# Frostings and Icings

## Vanilla or Mint Icing

2 cups confectioner's or powdered sugar

1 teaspoon GF vanilla or mint extract

3 tablespoons milk

Combine all ingredients until smooth, adding more milk one tablespoon at a time to desired consistency.

## Brown Sugar Frosting

¼ cup butter

½ cup brown sugar

3 cups confectioner's or powdered sugar

¼ cup brewed coffee, cooled

In a mixer, beat the butter and brown sugar until smooth. Slowly add the confectioners sugar and coffee, beating constantly until creamy.

## Fudge Icing and Buttercream Frosting

Recipes page 132

# *Whipped Cream*

To make fresh whipped cream, use 1 cup of heavy whipping cream and 1 teaspoon GF vanilla extract.  Put your mixing bowl and whisk in the freezer for about 20-30 minutes before making the whipped cream.  Make sure the heavy cream is also well chilled.  Start your mixer on low speed and gradually increase to higher speeds. Making the cream by hand will take at least 4-5 minutes of constant whisking.

*Chocolate Whipped Cream:*  Add 2 tablespoons cocoa powder and 2 teaspoons confectioner's sugar

*Maple Whipped Cream:*  As cream thickens, slowly drizzle ¼ cup maple syrup into the bowl and continue to whisk

*Cinnamon Whipped Cream:*  Add 1 teaspoon cinnamon and 3 tablespoons confectioner's sugar

*Kahlua and Cream:*  Add 3 tablespoons confectioner's sugar and 3 tablespoons Kahlua liquor

*You can also substitute equal amounts of almond or mint extract for the vanilla extract.*

To keep the consistency of the whipped cream if you need to make it ahead of time, add 2 tablespoons instant vanilla pudding mix while whisking.

# Pie Crusts

### Corn Flake Crust

5 cups GF corn flakes

4 tablespoons butter, melted

1 tablespoon sugar

·1 teaspoon cinnamon (optional)

The corn flakes should make about 2 cups of fine crumbs. Melt the butter and stir together with the corn flake crumbs and cinnamon. Press along the bottom and side of a 9 inch pie plate or springform pan.

### Coconut Crust

1 (7oz.) bag shredded coconut

2 tablespoons butter

Rub the butter along the bottom and sides of a 9 inch pie plate or a springform pan. Press the coconut into the pan.

### Almond or Pecan Crust

2 ½ cups finely ground almonds or pecans

2 tablespoons sugar

4 tablespoons butter, melted

Mix all ingredients until they are well combined. Press into the bottom of a 9 inch pie plate or springform pan.

# Cookie Crumb Crust

2 cups finely crushed GF cookies

½ cup butter, melted

Mix the cookie crumbs with butter until well combined.  Press into the bottom of a 9 inch pie plate or springform pan.  Use any of your favorite GF cookies including:

GF gingersnaps

GF arrowroot cookies

GF animal crackers

GF chocolate cookies

GF graham crackers

GF shortbread cookies

# Other Sweets and Snacks

# Soft Pretzels

3 ½ cups GF flour

3 teaspoons xanthan gum

1 teaspoon GF baking powder

1 tablespoon brown sugar

2 teaspoons salt (preferably Sea Salt)

1 tablespoon yeast, dissolved in 1 cup lukewarm water)

2 teaspoons baking soda

4 cups water

1 egg, beaten

Allow the yeast and water mix to sit for 10 minutes. In a large bowl, mix the yeast/water, brown sugar and salt together. Add the GF flour, xanthan gum and baking powder and mix until the dough is smooth. Knead until the dough comes together in a smooth ball. Cover the bowl, place in a warm spot and allow it to double in size. Divide the dough into 8 equal sections. Roll each piece into a rope (slightly thicker than a pencil). Each rope will make 2 pretzels. Twist each section into a pretzel shape and place on a baking sheet. Cover with plastic wrap in a warm place and let sit for 45-60 minutes.

Preheat oven to 450°. In a medium saucepan, bring 4 cups of water and baking soda to a boil. Drop each pretzel carefully into the water and boil for 1 minute. Remove with a slotted spoon and return to the baking sheet. Brush with the beaten egg and bake for 12-15 minutes. Top with sea salt, cinnamon or parmesan cheese immediately out of the oven. Can also be frozen and reheated in the oven or microwave.

# Cheddar Crackers

1 cup GF flour

¼ teaspoon xanthan gum

4 tablespoons butter

1 ½ cups grated sharp cheddar cheese

¾ teaspoon salt

½ teaspoon pepper

3-4 tablespoons water

¼ cup parmesan cheese

In a food processor or mixer, mix together the GF flour, xanthan gum, butter, salt cheddar cheese, salt and pepper. Add the water 1 tablespoon at a time until the dough forms a ball. Wrap in plastic wrap and chill for at least 1 hour.

Preheat oven to 350°. On a surface dusted with GF flour or cornmeal, roll out the dough to ¼ inch thickness. Cut into squares or shapes with a pizza cutter or cookie cutter. Bake on a cookie sheet lightly sprayed with GF cooking spray for 15-20 minutes. Sprinkle with parmesan cheese immediately out of the oven. Cool completely and store in an airtight container.

# Baked Bananas and Pineapple

3 medium ripe bananas

1 (8oz.) can crushed pineapple

3 tablespoons sugar or 2 ½ tablespoons honey

1 tablespoon lemon juice

1 ½ teaspoon corn starch

1 tablespoon butter

Preheat oven to 350°. Melt the butter in the bottom of an 8x8 inch pan. Drain the pineapples, reserving the liquid, and place them on the bottom of the baking dish. Peel and slice the bananas and place them in a single layer over the pineapples. Mix the corn starch, honey or sugar and pineapple juice together. Pour over the bananas and pineapple. Bake for 20 minutes.

# Apple Crisp

5-6 medium apples, peeled and cored

2 tablespoons lemon juice

½ cup GF flour

¼ cup brown sugar

¼ cup granulated sugar

¼ cup butter

½ teaspoon salt

1 teaspoon cinnamon

½ teaspoon nutmeg

Preheat oven to 350°. Slice the apples and place them in a medium bowl, mixing with the lemon juice. Combine the GF flour, brown sugar, granulated sugar, butter, salt, cinnamon and nutmeg until well blended. Stir half of the mixture with the sliced apples and pour into an 8x8 inch baking dish. Pour the remaining mixture over the top of the apples. Bake for 30 minutes or until the apples are tender. Serve warm or cold.

# Applesauce

8-9 medium apples

2 teaspoons cinnamon

½ teaspoon nutmeg

Juice of 1 lemon

½ cup brown sugar

¼ cup granulated sugar

1 cup apple juice

Peel, core and slice the apples. In a large saucepan, combine all of the ingredients adding enough water to cover the apples. Bring to a boil, reduce heat to low and simmer for 30 minutes or until apples are tender. Remove from heat and mash with a potato masher. Serve hot or cold.

# Quinoa Pudding

1 cup quinoa*

2 cups water

2 eggs

½ cup sugar

½ teaspoon salt

2 cups milk

½ cup raisins

½ cup chopped apples

½ cup finely chopped walnut (optional)

1 teaspoon GF vanilla

1/8 teaspoon nutmeg

½ teaspoon cinnamon

Preheat oven to 350°. In a medium saucepan heat the quinoa and water to a boil. Reduce heat to low, cover and simmer over low heat for 15 minutes. Drain any excess liquid and allow to cool slightly. In a small saucepan, heat the milk until it just comes to a boil. Stir in the quinoa and remove from heat. Whisk together the eggs, sugar and salt, nutmeg, cinnamon and vanilla. Slowly stir in the milk and quinoa and mix well. Stir in the apples, raisins and walnuts. Pour into an oven-proof casserole dish and bake for 60-75 minutes, or until set.

*Before using quinoa, rinse well in cold water. You may also substitute 2 cups of cooked rice in recipe and omit quinoa and water.

# Peanut Brittle

2 cups sugar

1 cup light corn syrup

1 tablespoon butter

1 ½ cups salted nuts*

1 teaspoon baking soda

Butter or use GF cooking spray on a jelly roll pan or baking sheet with edges at least ½ inch high.  In a medium saucepan over low-medium heat, combine the sugar, corn syrup and butter until boiling.  Stirring constantly, add the nuts and continue cooking until the mixture turns golden in color.  Stir in baking soda and continue stirring until the mixture turns a deep brown color.  Pour into pan and cool completely.  Break into pieces and store in an airtight container.

*Use peanuts, almonds, walnuts, pecans or a mix of nuts

# *Baked Pumpkin Pudding*

2 eggs, beaten

1 can (16 oz.) pumpkin

¼ cup brown sugar

½ teaspoon cinnamon

1/8 teaspoon ginger

1/8 teaspoon cloves

1/8 teaspoon nutmeg

1 (12 oz.) can evaporated skim milk

¼ cup coarsely chopped walnuts (optional)

Preheat oven to 325°. Stir together the eggs, pumpkin, brown sugar, cinnamon, cloves, ginger and nutmeg until well blended. Stir in the milk and pour into 6 (6oz.) custard dishes or one large oven-proof dish. Place dishes into a larger baking dish and pour water around the custard dishes up to 1 inch high. Bake for 50 minutes or until set (longer if using one large baking dish.). Sprinkle with walnuts.

# Fruit Tart

*Meringue Shell:*

4 egg whites

1/8 teaspoon salt

¼ teaspoon cream of tartar

1 cup sugar

1 teaspoon GF vanilla

*Filling:*

1 (14oz.) can sweetened condensed milk (not evaporated)

1 (8oz.) package cream cheese, softened

2 tablespoons lemon juice

*Topping:*

2 cups sliced fresh peaches, strawberries, blueberries, kiwis, raspberries or a combination

Preheat oven to 275°. Lightly spray a 9 inch pie plate with GF cooking spray. Beat the egg whites and salt until frothy. Add the cream of tartar and continue beating until soft peaks form. Add the sugar slowly, beating until the mixture is thick and glossy. Stir in the vanilla. Spread around the bottom and sides of the pie plate, making a rim around the edges. The sides should be about 1 inch thick and the bottom should be about ½ inch thick. Bake for 40-45 minutes until it is slightly dry, being careful not to brown the meringue. Loosen while warm, but leave in the pie plate to cool completely.

In a food processor or mixer, blend together the cream cheese, sweetened condensed milk and lemon juice until smooth. Pour into cooled meringue crust and refrigerate for one hour, or until firm. Top with sliced fruit.

# Pear Clafoutis

1 tablespoon butter

4 large pears*

¾ cup brown sugar

2 eggs

2 tablespoons GF flour

1 cup milk

1 teaspoon GF vanilla

½ teaspoon cinnamon

1/8 teaspoon salt

Preheat oven to 350°. Melt the butter in an 8x8 inch baking dish. Peel and thinly slice the pears and layer in the bottom of the baking dish. Beat the eggs until frothy, add the sugar and continue beating until the eggs thicken. Add the flour, milk, vanilla, cinnamon and salt and mix until combined. Pour over the pears and bake for 35-40 minutes, or until the pears are tender.

*Do not mix varieties of pears, as they will not finish baking at the same time.

# *Tipsy Fruit*

1 small cantaloupe, cubed

1 cup watermelon chunks

3 peaches, cut into 1 inch chunks

3 apples, cut into 1 inch chunks

1 cup seedless grapes

2 cups rum

Combine the fruit and rum in a large bowl and refrigerate overnight. Drain the excess rum and put alternating pieces of fruit on bamboo skewers. Best served cold.

# Frozen Bananas

4 medium bananas

2 tablespoons butter

1 ½ cups GF milk chocolate chips

1 cup finely chopped peanuts (optional)

8 lollipop or popsicle sticks

Line a baking sheet with wax paper. Peel bananas and cut in half. Insert popsicle or lollipop sticks halfway into each banana. Freeze on baking sheet for at least 3 hours. Melt the chocolate and butter until smooth and pour into a tall narrow container or drinking glass. Dip each banana in chocolate, shaking off excess. Roll in peanuts and refreeze. Bananas will last in the freezer for up to 1 week.

# Fruit Smoothies

Blend all ingredients until smooth in a blender.

*Tofu Smoothie:*
½ cup soft tofu
¼ cup lemon juice
½ banana, sliced
1 cup sliced peaches, raspberries or oranges
1 tablespoon honey

*Strawberry Banana Smoothie:*
1 cup plain yogurt
1 cup orange juice
1 cup strawberries, hulled and chopped
1 banana, sliced

*Blueberry Banana Smoothie:*
1 cup plain yogurt
½ cup milk (skim milk is OK)
1 cup blueberries (fresh or frozen)
1 banana, sliced

*Tropical Smoothie:*
½ cup canned coconut milk
½ cup plain yogurt
2 bananas, sliced
1 cup fresh or canned pineapple

# Bone Appétit
# Doggy Treats

# Veggie Biscuits

½ cup GF flour

½ cup cornmeal

¼ cup shredded cheese

½ cup vegetable oil

1 carrot, finely shredded

1 celery stalk, finely shredded

Preheat oven to 350°. Mix all ingredients until thoroughly combined. On a surface dusted with GF flour or cornmeal, roll out the dough to ¼ inch thick. Use a pizza cutter or cut into biscuit shapes. Place on a baking sheet and bake for 10-15 minutes. Turn off the oven and let cool completely in the oven.

**Gump**

# *Tuna Biscuits*

1 cup cornmeal

1 cup GF flour

¼ teaspoon baking powder

1 (6 oz.) can tuna in oil, undrained

1/3 cup water

1 tablespoon GF barbeque sauce

Preheat oven to 350°. Mix together the cornmeal, GF flour and baking powder. Stir in the tuna and oil and slowly add the water until the dough forms a ball. Roll out onto a surface dusted with GF flour or cornmeal to ¼ inch thick. Cut with a pizza cutter or cookie cutter. Bake for 20-25 minutes. Remove from oven and brush with barbeque sauce. Return to the oven (turned off) to cool completely.

**Divot**

# Peanut Butter Banana Bites

1 cup peanut butter
1 cup cornmeal
1 egg
¼ cup GF flour
½ ripe banana, mashed

Preheat oven to 350°.  Mix all ingredients together until they are well blended.  Form ½ inch balls and bake on an ungreased baking sheet for 10 minutes.  Turn the oven off and allow treats to cool completely.

**Bubba**

*"Digestion, of all the bodily functions, is the one which exercises the greatest influence on the mental state of an individual."*

*~Jean-Anthelme Brillat-Savarin*

# Index

# Hidden Sources of Gluten

Besides the commonly known foods such as bread, pasta, cookies, candies, and cakes, there are many hidden sources of gluten.  Some of them are listed below

Barley
Barley malt (a sweetener commonly used in breakfast cereals, snacks, and convenience foods)
Battered and breaded foods
Beer
Bird Seed
Bran
Brewers's yeast
Cereals: most contain malt flavoring, or some other non-GF ingredient
Chicken, vegetable and beef broths
Coloring
Couscous
Dairy Substitutes
Dog and cat food and treats
Dried meals and gravy mixes
Fillers
Flavorings
Graham flour
Grilled and fried restaurant food - gluten contaminated grill or grease
Ground spices - wheat flour is sometimes used to prevent clumping
Hydrolyzed plant protein
Hydrolyzed vegetable protein
Ice cream
Instant cocoa
Kamut
Lotions, creams and cosmetics
Low-fat/non-fat dairy products
Malt, including malted milk, malted liquor, etc.
Maltodextrin and dextrin (a common additive)
Matzo
Meats and meat products
Modified food starch
Mono- and diglycerides
Monosodium glutamate (MSG)
Packet & canned soups
Pie fillings
Prepared icings and frostings
Prescription and over-the counter medicines
Processed cheeses
Rice and soy beverages
Rye
Salad dressings
Sauce mixes and sauces (soy sauce, fish sauce, catsup, mustard, mayonnaise, etc)
Sauces, jams, gravies
Seitan
Semolina
Snack foods with added seasonings
Soy sauce (unless specified "wheat free")
Spelt
Spices
Stamps, envelopes, stickers or other gummed labels
Teriyaki and BBQ sauce
Textured vegetable protein

Thickeners and stabilizers
Toothpaste and mouthwash
Triticale
Udon
Vegetarian products (veggie burgers, etc.)

# Thank You

*Utica Fire Department- Station 2 (Bleecker St):*
For being the official gluten-free dessert taste-testers!

*Steve Reed:* For all your time and effort in taking the photographs for this book.

*Mike and Kathy Hanson:* For always checking in to see how things are going and for showing me that with a little creativity, there is always a way to accomplish any idea.

*My co-workers: Lisa Krantz and Pam Murray:* For being so kind while I was sick and for giving advice on every detail about the making of this cookbook. Now we can go back to talking about dogs, gardening and decorating!

*Anne Roland Lee:* For taking the time from your busy schedule to review the recipes in this book.

*My doctor, Dr. Garth Garramone of Digestive Disease Medicine of Central New York:* For listening to my concerns and for your persistence in finding the proper diagnosis.

*My sister-in-law, Dr. Barbara Ambrose:* For your wonderful ideas and editing skills for the cookbook and your concern and encouragement while I was sick.

*My dogs; Bubba, Gump and Divot:* The best (and smartest) "furkids" in the world!

Thank you to the friends and family who visited me in the hospital, called, and sent flowers and cards. You're concern meant more to me than you know. Also, thank you for your interest in learning about celiac disease and encouraging me to write this cookbook.

# Resources

American Dietetic Association
120 South Riverside Plaza, Suite 2000
Chicago, IL 60606-6995
Phone: 1-800-877-1600
Email: hotline@eatright.org
Internet: www.eatright.org

Celiac Disease Foundation
13251 Ventura Boulevard, #1
Studio City, CA 91604
Phone: 818-990-2354
Fax: 818-990-2379
Email: cdf@celiac.org
Internet: www.celiac.org

Celiac Sprue Association/USA Inc.
P.O. Box 31700
Omaha, NE 68131-0700
Phone: 1-877-272-4272 or 402-558-0600
Fax: 402-558-1347
Email: celiacs@csaceliacs.org
Internet: www.csaceliacs.org

Gluten Intolerance Group of North America
15110 10th Avenue, SW., Suite A
Seattle, WA 98166
Phone: 206-246-6652
Fax: 206-246-6531
Email: info@gluten.net
Internet: www.gluten.net

Gluten-Free Living (a bimonthly newsletter)
P.O. Box 105
Hastings-on-Hudson, NY 10706
Phone: 914-969-2018
Email: gfliving@aol.com

National Foundation for Celiac Awareness
124 South Maple Street
Ambler, PA 19002
Phone: 215-325-1306
Email: info@celiacawareness.org
Internet: www.celiacawareness.org

North American Society for Pediatric Gastroenterology, Hepatology and Nutrition (NASPGHAN)
Flourtown, PA 19031
Phone: 215-233-0808
Email: naspghan@naspghan.org
Internet: www.naspghan.org www.cdhnf.org

# *About the Author*

Julie Ambrose is a registered dental hygienist in central New York. She is currently developing an educational program for dental hygiene students on Celiac Disease. The program has already been requested by over 90 dental hygiene schools across the country and will raise awareness of the symptoms and appropriate treatment of celiac patients in the dental office.

A portion of the proceeds from each book will go to the author's favorite charities to benefit animal welfare and adoption organizations and celiac disease awareness.

For any questions or comments about the book or for more information about celiac disease as it relates to dental care, you may contact the author at

www.WithoutTheWheat.com